How to Teach Students Who *Don't* Look Like You

To all the teachers who take risks to improve their classroom instruction and passionately believe that ALL children can achieve

How to Teach Students Who *Don't* Look Like You

Culturally Relevant Teaching Strategies

Bonnie M. Davis

CORWIN PRESS
A SAGE Publications Company
Thousand Oaks, California

For information:

Corwin Press
A Sage Publications Company
2455 Teller Road
Thousand Oaks, California 91320
E-mail: order@corwinpress.com

Sage Publications Ltd.
1 Oliver's Yard
55 City Road
London EC1Y 1SP
United Kingdom

Sage Publications India Pvt. Ltd.
B-42, Panchsheel Enclave
Post Box 4109
New Delhi 110 017 India

Printed in the United States of America.

Library of Congress Cataloging-in-Publication Data

Davis, Bonnie M.
How to teach students who don't look like you : culturally relevant teaching strategies/by Bonnie M. Davis.
        p. cm.
Includes bibliographical references and index.
ISBN: 978-1-4129-2446-7 (cloth) — ISBN: 978-1-4129-2447-4 (pbk.)
   1. Multicultural education—United States. 2. Minorities—Education—United States. 3. School environment—United States. 4. Pluralism (Social sciences)—United States. I. Title.
LC1099.3.D395 2006
370.117—dc22   2005019388

This book is printed on acid-free paper.

10 11 12   11 10 9

Acquisitions Editor:	Rachel Livsey
Editorial Assistant:	Phyllis Cappello
Project Editor:	Tracy Alpern
Copy Editor:	Barbara Coster
Proofreader:	Penelope Sippel
Typesetter:	C&M Digitals (P) Ltd.
Indexer:	Sylvia Coates
Cover Designer:	Rose Storey
Graphic Designer:	Lisa Miller

Contents

Preface

Do you

- search for strategies to close the achievement gap?
- seek to understand the cultural differences of your students?
- look for lessons to motivate and support diverse learners?

If you are like many teachers, you continue to look for ways to improve your classroom instruction. As a classroom teacher with more than 35 years of experience, I, too, was always searching for new strategies, understandings, and lessons to support the changing population of students who yearly entered my classroom.

This book is a result of that search. It is an organic document, one that can continue to grow as you interact with the book and your colleagues.

The chapters take you through the following stages:

- A general recognition of culture and how it shapes the lens through which you view the world
- An examination of research on diverse learners
- A discussion of the achievement gap
- The personal narratives and racial histories of two educators
- Strategies to build an environment for learning
- Research-based instructional strategies (K–12) to implement across the disciplines, with a focus on literacy
- An achievement support group model
- Suggestions for professional development
- A selected bibliography pertaining to diverse learners

You can read the chapters in the above sequence, or you can open the book anywhere and read an individual chapter, much like a book of short stories tied together by a common theme. You can read and respond in the book, using it as a private book study and a professional development tool. Or you can use it with your staff and colleagues during professional development opportunities (find PD suggestions in the Facilitator's Guide at the back of the book). The chapters are educator friendly and are meant to be discussed and responded to informally and honestly. The research, strategies, and culturally responsive classroom lessons found in the book are designed to support and improve the academic achievement of diverse learners.

How did you learn what you know about teaching? I learned what I know about teaching from men in a prison, women in a homeless shelter, and affluent middle schoolers, as well as high school and college students in suburban and urban areas. The men taught me that even though the common denominator in our prisons is "poverty," poverty does not equate to a lack of intelligence. Some of the most intelligent and best writers I taught were these men. The women in the homeless shelter taught me that our students must find and share their voices in the classroom, for when we allow students to find their voices, their writing glows. All too often students in our society lack this opportunity, and they sometimes find less productive means of screaming who they are. And scores of middle schoolers from an affluent school district taught me that it was not enough to walk into their classroom with a doctorate in English and more than 20 years of teaching experience at the high school and college levels—these children demanded instruction that challenged and engaged them. No longer could lectures grab and keep their attention. I had to learn what I didn't know I didn't know about good instruction. This book focuses on students who may not look like you, may not come from similar backgrounds, and may not approach learning like you. Just as the student populations I have taught have informed my instruction, your students speak to you with their needs (or perhaps they scream at you with their needs). Your life experiences add to your teaching repertoire.

Who are diverse learners? They are the homeless children, the migrant children, the immigrant children learning English, children dealing with gender issues, children with learning disabilities, special needs children, and children from diverse cultures—students perhaps not previously included or successful in our classrooms.

To provide diverse learners with culturally responsive instruction, we must build relationships and hold high expectations, provide rigorous content knowledge while making explicit the hidden rules of learning, and teach students how to learn as well as what to learn.

While addressing these educational goals, this book

- shares the research,
- gives examples that support the research,
- suggests questions to ask about your instructional practice,
- presents concrete strategies to implement in your classroom,
- offers reflections for professional growth.

In addition, the book offers you a unique opportunity. Unlike many excellent books in the marketplace that give research-based instructional strategies, this book includes a section that focuses on race and privilege and its impact upon two female educators: one Black American and one White American. Reading their stories (Chapters 5 and 6) gives you a glimpse into the racial complexities of their educational landscape and examines a topic seldom found in educational literature. These two chapters are designed not for the timid but for educators ready and willing to examine privilege in our society and continue a journey of cultural proficiency.

As you read, consider setting goals. For example, you may wish to read this book in order to improve instruction or make your instruction more culturally responsive: your end result may be improved student achievement; your action plan may include one chapter per week of study and application; and your target date may be the end of your next academic semester. Setting goals tunes our brain to focus on our needs and to filter out the rest.

I invite you to join in a professional conversation as you read, study, and reflect your way through the book, and I welcome your comments and suggestions. You may e-mail me at a4achievement@earthlink.net.

Who this book is for:

- First and foremost, this book is for teachers from a teacher. The information and strategies are for preservice teachers, beginning teachers, veteran teachers—all of us.
- Principals at every level who wish to enhance the knowledge base of their staff and provide opportunities for collegial dialogue and learning
- Professional development chairs, supervisors, mentors, and coaches whose job it is to encourage teachers and provide culturally responsive materials for them
- Professional learning communities, whether they be a group of 2 or 200
- College and university instructors and their students in preservice and graduate courses where students need or require information on diverse learners
- Central office administrators engaged in a districtwide endeavor to become more culturally proficient and to close the gap

Enjoy!

Acknowledgments

All students have a story to tell, and given the right conditions and teacher support, I believe they will share their stories with us. This book shares the story of my teaching life, a life that would not have existed were it not for the support of countless educators. To all of you, I say, "Thank you!" For believing in me in a special way, I thank Robert Hamblin, Charles I. Rankin, Linda Henke, Julie Heifetz, John Bierk, Elizabeth Krekeler, Jere Hochman, Louella Huckeby, Manuel Davis, and Nancy Saguto. I send special gratitude and hugs to my friend Dorothy Kelly for including her story in this book.

I owe a huge debt to my sister Ruth Dambach, who guided me through the preparation of this book, and to my friend Kim Anderson for the publication of my earlier book.

Working with people who trust and support you is an immense gift in life. Dennis Lubeck, Sheila Onuska, Sue Heggarty, Megan Moncure, and Michael Grady of the International Education Consortium have done this for me. The IEC's story mirrors excellence in professional development over the decades. Thank you!

My family's stories are woven of many threads. I thank my father, Homer Schnurbusch, for his lifetime of love and support. I am thankful for my mother's love and selfless devotion to our family. I am grateful to my sisters, Susan Welker, Ruth Dambach, and Mary Aldredge, and their families, for their adult friendship and love. I thank my children, Leah and Reeve, for who they are and especially for who they have become. I never dreamed one's adult children could bring so much joy.

I thank Fred Baugh, my partner and my best friend for 15 years. Your story is yet to tell. You are my Buckaroo Banzai.

Were it not for the folks at Corwin Press, you would not be reading this book. A special thanks to the Corwin team in charge of editorial and production processes: to Rachel Livsey, acquisitions editor, for encouraging me to send her my writing; to Phyllis Cappello, editorial assistant, for making sure that you, the reader, found access to this book; and to Tracy Alpern, project editor, for pulling together the production of the book. With Barbara Coster, copy editor, added to the mix, I felt completely supported throughout this process. These four ladies were always available by phone and e-mail with kind and gentle responses, even when I asked ignorant questions. They modeled what a teacher should do when her student engages in a completely new learning process.

The contributions of the following reviewers are gratefully acknowledged:

Kathy Hansen
BTSA Induction Program Specialist
Kern County Superintendent of
    Schools
Bakersfield, CA

Concha Delgado Gaitan
Independent Writer and Researcher
San Francisco Bay Area

Kikanza Nuri Robins
Organizational Development
    Consultant
www.kikanzanurirobins.com
Los Angeles, CA

Diane M. Holben
Director of Research, Planning, and
    Accountability
Allentown School District
Allentown, PA

Arlene Myslinski
ESL Teacher
Buffalo Grove High School
Buffalo Grove, IL

Molly Burger
Principal
Middleton Middle School
Middleton, ID

Sherry Maddox-Adams
Executive Director
Life Academy
Atlanta, GA

Mariela Nunez-Janes
Assistant Professor,
    Anthropology
Co-Director, Ethnic Studies
University of North Texas
Denton, TX

Rosalind Pijeaux Hale
Professor, Division of Education
Xavier University of Louisiana
New Orleans, LA

Tery J. Medina
Associate Director
Southeastern Equity Center
Fort Lauderdale, FL

About the Author

 **Bonnie M. Davis, PhD**, is a veteran teacher of 37 years who is passionate about education. She has taught in middle schools, high schools, universities, homeless shelters, and a men's prison. She is the recipient of numerous awards, including Teacher of the Year, the Governor's Award for Excellence in Teaching, and the Anti-Defamation League's World of Difference Community Service Award. She has presented at numerous national conferences and provides services to schools through her consulting firm, A4Achievement. Her publications include *African-American Academic Achievement: Building a Classroom of Excellence* and numerous articles on literacy instruction.

She received her BS in education, her MA in English, her MAI in communications, and her PhD in English. She may be reached at www.a4achievement.net or by e-mail at a4achievement@earthlink.net.

PART I

Building Background Knowledge About Diverse Learners

1

Our Culture

The Way We View the World

What do you see when you enter your school? If you are like many teachers, you see a sea of smiling faces, some that look like yours and others that don't. This book offers you an opportunity to read and think about those children who may not look or even think like you. The first three chapters in the book build background knowledge about culture, diverse learners, and the achievement gap. The next three examine our inner selves and our inner worlds. The remainder of the book looks at the learning environment and classroom instruction. This book combines the affective and the cognitive, the what and the who of teaching, the external and the internal worlds in which we live and work. Let's begin with the children you see when you walk into your school.

Describe the children in your school.

_____

_____

_____

Describe the faculty/staff in your school.

_____

_____

_____

Describe yourself.

_____

_____

_____

OUR CULTURAL LENS

If you picked up this book, you probably teach a diverse group of children. This chapter will offer you an opportunity to examine your cultural lens and reflect upon how culture impacts our daily lives. Our culture is the lens through which we view the world. By better understanding our own cultural lens, we may better realize the importance of honoring the cultures of each student in our classrooms. In the following chapters, you will find numerous strategies that honor the diverse cultures found in our schools.

We can't deny that our children are changing in complexion and complexity, and you may find yearly more children in your classroom who don't look like you or each other. As educators, we have more opportunities than ever to learn about each other and to share our cultural knowledge with our students.

Nearly 40% of U.S. citizens are members of racial and ethnic minorities, with approximately 35 million, or 13% Latino/a/Hispanic, 12% African American, 4% Asian American, 1% American Indian or Alaska Native, and 8% other racial/minority groups. These numbers are reflected in our public schools. In 1998, out of 47 million public school students, almost 40% were children from linguistic and culturally diverse backgrounds. Nearly 10 million children come from homes where a language other than English is spoken, and the language minority population will soon outnumber the English-speaking population in more than 50 major cities in the United States (Artiles & Ortiz, 2002).

What does this mean for you? Are you equipped to teach children whose culture differs from your own? Professionals today must examine their own culture and its inherent values, consider the different cultures and values of their students and the students' families, and explore how to meet the needs of each student by acknowledging, respecting, and accommodating the culture and value system of the family (Artiles & Ortiz, 2002). Examining our culture is one place to begin.

Each of us views the world through a unique lens. Each lens is composed of a diverse spectrum that includes many facets of our lives. Think of it as a pair of glasses that allows you to see the world differently from every other person who inhabits it. Every other person wears a lens that colors his or her own view. This individual way of looking at the world is our individual perspective through which we judge events and people around us. Our heredity, environment, and previous experiences comprise our world view.

WHAT IS CULTURE?

Culture is *the totality of ideas, beliefs, values, activities, and knowledge of a group or individuals who share historical, geographical, religious, racial, linguistic, ethnic, or social traditions, and who transmit, reinforce, and modify those traditions.*

A culture is the total of everything an individual learns by growing up in a particular context and results in a set of expectations for appropriate behavior in seemingly similar contexts.

In their book *Cultural Proficiency: A Manual for School Leaders,* Lindsey, Nuri Robins, and Terrell (2003) define culture as "everything you do that enables you to identify with people who are like you and that distinguishes you from people who differ from you" (p. 41). They state that culture is about groupness because a culture is a "group of people identified by their shared history, values, and patterns of behavior" (p. 41).

Culture provides us with a blueprint of the "hidden rules" of our group, a map for living that offers consistency and predictability in our everyday actions (Lindsey et al., 2003). These hidden rules are known as cultural expectations. Cultural expectations help us keep outsiders outside and insiders controlled (Lindsey et al., 2003), thereby sustaining our group culture. We learn cultural expectations through the process of acculturation.

Acculturation is *the process whereby the culture, values, and patterns of the majority are adopted by a person or an ethnic, social, religious affiliation, language, or national group.*

I was born and acculturated into a nuclear two-parent family that was White, middle class, small town, midwestern, Catholic, and conservative. These parameters formed the young adult lens I used to view the world.

What was your young adult lens?

_____

_____

_____

_____

Describe your culture today. Which parts of your young adult lens still describe you (several of mine have changed)?

_____

_____

_____

_____

CULTURALLY PROFICIENT

We weave in and out of several kinds of cultures during our day. To become culturally proficient in each of these, we may need to widen our understanding of culture (Lindsey et al., 2003). Cultural proficiency is the *"policies and practices of a school or the values and behaviors of an individual that enable the person or school to interact effectively in a culturally diverse environment"* (Lindsey et al., 2003, pp. xix–xx; emphasis added). It is an "approach," not a theory, program, or silver bullet. This does not mean you must know everything there is to know about others. That is impossible. Rather, it means that "you have the self-awareness to recognize how you—because of your ethnicity, your culture, and your life experiences—may offend or otherwise affect others," as well as what you offer to others (Nuri Robins, Lindsey, Lindsey, & Terrell, 2002, p. xii). Being culturally proficient allows you to use "teachable moments" to share yourself and learn from others (Nuri Robins et al., 2002, p. xii).

ORGANIZATIONAL CULTURE

Your school consists of several cultures. You work in an occupational culture and an organizational culture. Your occupational culture, if you are an educator, is education, and educators often share beliefs, dress, and language (jargon sometimes referred to as "educationalese"), in addition to other factors.

Your organizational culture is your district and your school site. Even within your district, you will find school cultures that differ. Elementary, middle, and high school cultures differ. Each school differs from other schools in a district, yet they share some commonalities because they are in the same district. For example, the neighborhoods that surround the schools may be similar, influencing the schools' culture, or they may vary economically, influencing the schools' culture. If you teach in an elementary school, you may find more in common culturally with teachers who work in elementary schools in other districts than the teachers who teach at the high school in your district. In one district, teachers may work hours in their buildings at the end of the school day; in another district, teachers may be out the doors as soon as the buses leave (and sometimes before). There is a difference in the "work" culture between the two.

Think about a "coffee/tea" culture. Does your faculty lounge offer coffee or tea to teachers? If so, do you pay for it? Who makes it daily? Which teachers drink it? Who cleans up the drink station? In visiting schools, a substitute may find a wide range of coffee/tea cultures. In some schools, there is free coffee/tea, the staff drinks it, and someone is assigned to make the coffee/tea and clean up the area. In other schools, there is none. Between these two, there are schools where coffee/tea duties are rotated through the staff, the staff chips in to pay for the services, gourmet coffees/teas are available, staff is allowed to take the drinks into their classrooms, and so on. However, substitutes coming into the building need to know the "hidden rules" of the coffee/tea culture at the school if they want to participate in the coffee/tea culture. They may need their own cup or correct change to participate in the school ritual, and if they find themselves without a cup or cash, they may find no one willing to assist their acculturation into the school's coffee/tea culture. Cultural expectations function in much the same way. If we do not know the expectations (hidden rules or codes) of the cultural setting, we may find ourselves unable to participate in the culture.

ETHNIC CULTURE

To many, culture refers to racial or ethnic differences. Ethnic culture results from our ancestral heritage and geography, common histories, and physical appearance (Lindsey et al., 2003). My ethnic culture is White American. Dorothy's, whose racial history is found in Chapter 5, is Black American. We share an American culture, but our lenses differ in that she views and lives her world as a Black person in this American culture and I live and view my life as a White person in this American culture. However, we share an identical nationality. Nationality means place of origin (Singleton, 2003). For many of us, our nationality is the United States.

What is your ethnicity?

_____

_____

_____

_____

What is your nationality?

_____

_____

_____

_____

How does your culture, ethnicity, and nationality differ from your students and colleagues?

_____

_____

_____

_____

Think about the way you view your world. What factors contribute to the lens you wear as you view the world?

_____

_____

_____

_____

CULTURAL FACTORS

Below are several major factors that influence the way we see our world and contribute to the many cultures we weave in and out of each day:

- Family
- Gender
- Race
- Age
- Sexual orientation
- Language
- Friends
- Religion
- School
- Geography
- Income of family/social class
- Political views
- Ethnicity
- Electronic media
- Social organizations
- Others

When we interact with our students or colleagues, we bring the baggage of our past experiences, our prejudices, our preferences, as well as those of our families, and other factors that influence the lens through which we view the world. Those we face bring the same.

Examine the list above. Which ones do you share with your students and/or colleagues? For example, your district may be comprised largely of Protestants, and you are Protestant; therefore, you share religion in common with your staff and students.

_____

_____

_____

In which ones do you differ from your students and/or colleagues?

_____

_____

_____

The more differences you find, the more bridges you may need to build to reach those in your daily work lives.

What have you learned as a result of defining your culture?

_____

_____

_____

FRAMEWORK OF CULTURAL PROFICIENCY

One effective way to build bridges to cultures that differ from ours is to use a framework of cultural proficiency when we interact with others. Using a framework of cultural proficiency supports our becoming culturally proficient educators. We can embark on a journey to become culturally proficient educators to meet the needs of each student by acknowledging, respecting, and accommodating the culture and value system of the family (Artiles & Ortiz, 2002).

How do we do this? Even though there is no magic formula, the magic will occur when "faculty use the cultural proficiency model to guide inquiry and response to the issues caused by diversity within themselves and within their schools" (Lindsey et al., 2003, p. xxi). When finding ourselves in a new cultural setting, we must know how to determine what we need to know about the other cultures in an inoffensive manner and know what we need to teach others about ourselves (Lindsey et al., 2003). Consider using the books cited at the end of this chapter to guide your staff in examining the issues of diversity in your school.

We begin this journey by learning about ourselves. A book study is one tool to do that. Professional development that examines cultural proficiency is another. The exercise that follows might be used in a staff meeting or professional development opportunity as a tool to learn about other staff members. Each time I have used this activity with students and adults, the results have been overwhelmingly positive. The result has always been that any two individuals find that they have more commonalities than differences. This exercise underscores our humanity.

Suggested Exercise:

- Pair off with another staff member.

- Use a Venn diagram

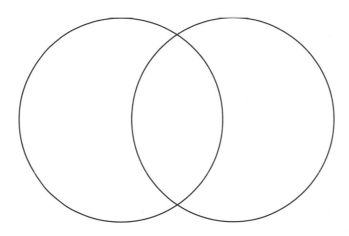

- Write your name above one circle of the Venn diagram; your partner writes his or her name above the other.

- Fill out the Venn diagram with your similarities and differences. For example, if you are of different genders, your gender would go in your own circle. If you share gender, your gender would be in the overlapping part of your circles. Fill in your Venn diagrams with as many aspects of your lives as time allows.

- Share with the larger group. You tell about your partner. Your partner tells about you. Share your similarities however you choose. Adults and students find creative ways to share during this exercise as it creates a community of learners.

CULTURAL HOMOGENEITIES

If you are fortunate to have different cultural groups as part of your staff, check for cultural homogeneities. Cultural homogeneities are *similarities that exist within cultural groups.* For example, Deborah Tannen's (1990) work in communication styles finds that women's and men's communication styles differ because of gender. Each gender possesses its own culture.

You may find that your different cultural groups share cultural homogeneities about which you were unaware. Learning about the cultural homogeneities of other groups in our school setting increases our awareness of culture. Female appearance is one example of where you can observe cultural homogeneities. In some female cultural groups, long fingernails painted in elaborate patterns are the rage; in others, short, unpolished nails are the norm. Tattoos are a popular homogeneity of some groups of young people. Even text messaging is a homogeneity among some groups of young professionals. These are current fads or practices, but it is possible to find cultural homogeneities that span generations and demographic areas. During a diversity workshop, African Americans and an Afro-Haitian (who said she learned the shared cultural homogeneities growing up in Haiti) found that they shared the cultural homogeneities of some terms unknown to the White participants. These terms included *my kitchen* for describing a place on their heads and *the hawk* for describing the wind, as well as others. Two books that offer specific information about cultural homogeneities of Blacks and Whites are the following:

It's the Little Things: Everyday Interactions That Anger, Annoy, and Divide the Races by Lena Williams, an African American who is a 25-year veteran of the *New York Times*

Afraid of the Dark: What Whites and Blacks Need to Know About Each Other by Jim Myers, a White man married to a Black woman, who was the chief writer for a *USA Today* series on race

If you plan to use these books in a book study with staff, you may want to have a skilled facilitator to lead the groups.

Viewed as an adventure and a journey, the road to cultural proficiency is a lifelong endeavor that may energize your school, both staff and students.

Try the following strategies and don't forget to share them with your students.

Level: Elementary/Middle/High School/Adult
Subject: Cross-curricular

- Attend art events given by or about people of other cultures. Great art is found in every culture, and art is a great equalizer.
- Become friends with people of other cultures.
- Live in integrated neighborhoods.
- Enroll your children in integrated schools.
- Read the literature of other cultures.
- Build a culturally responsive learning climate in your classroom that respects diversity.
- Use language daily in your classroom that values diversity so that your students can begin to model your language. For example, talk about the important contributions of cultural groups, such as the contribution of the Africans to mathematics.
- Bring in newspapers and magazines of diverse cultures and have them out and available for students to peruse.
- Read newspaper articles to your class that foster positive portraits of diverse groups.
- Post simple phrases in multiple languages throughout your classroom and school.
- Post role models of diverse people throughout your school.
- Share the poetry of other cultures in your classroom. You could begin class by reading a poem by a culturally diverse poet. Before class, privately ask a student who shares that culture if he or she would like to read it to the class.

- Study a foreign language.
- Ask your students to write about their family customs and discuss them in your classes.
- Ask your students to do the Venn diagram exercise with members of the class.
- Ask your students to bring in a family dish to share on a special day.
- Don't privilege one culture above another. For example, "privileging" one group occurs when a teacher calls more often on one group of students, uses examples from the lives of one cultural group more than others, and so on. In the 1950s, in the culturally homogenous elementary school classroom, we called these "teacher's pets."
- Respect the traditions of other cultures.
- Don't make assumptions about the rituals or practices of other cultures.
- Always ask yourself how you would feel if the cultural situation were reversed. For example, what if schools decided not to honor Christmas. How would you feel if you were Christian? How would you feel if you were Jewish or Muslim? What if nearly all senators in our U.S. Senate were women? How would you feel? What if your entire central office administration were a different cultural group from yours? How would you feel? Often, we take for granted the cultural dominance of a group without thinking about how it might feel if a different cultural group held that domination.
- Travel, travel, travel—forgo the tours and travel so that you have the opportunity to meet and talk with the locals, wherever you go.

Think about what you have read and reflected upon in this chapter. Are you interested in adopting a culturally proficient framework for your work? If so, what might be your first steps?

_____

_____

_____

This first chapter examined our personal lens in preparation for learning about and understanding the lenses of our students. Since each of us "sees" the world in a unique way, the more we can learn about the cultures of others, the more we can understand the reasons why our students make the choices they make and do the things they do in our classrooms. Chapter 2 includes research on diverse students that directly impacts student achievement.

❖   ❖   ❖

SUGGESTED READING

Artiles, Alfredo J., and Alba A. Ortiz, eds. 2002. *English Language Learners With Special Education Needs.*

Lindsey, Randall. 2005. *The Culturally Proficient School: An Implementation Guide for School Leaders.*

Lindsey, Randall, et al. 2003. *Cultural Proficiency: A Manual for School Leaders.*

Nuri Robins, Kikanza, et al. 2002. *Culturally Proficient Instruction: A Guide for People Who Teach.*

2

Understanding Diverse Learners

Diverse learners enter our classrooms with a diversity of experiences. They may differ from you and each other in ethnicity, race, socioeconomic status, gender, learning modalities, cognitive development, and social development (Tileston, 2004). This chapter examines some of the diverse academic experiences that our students encounter and offers strategies to use in your classrooms. In no way does this research comprehensively cover all groups of diverse learners; however, the strategies employed in this chapter and throughout this book are often cited as effective for students in each of the groups stated above.

Our job as teachers is to reach and teach them all. What might seem an overwhelming task can be better accomplished through understanding our diverse learners, knowing that they often practice different communication styles from the dominant culture (Nieto, 2000), may need different teaching strategies from the dominant culture (Marzano, 2004), may require a relationship with you, the teacher, before they decide to learn from you (Haycock, 2001), and may be confronting personal issues about which you are unfamiliar.

Some of the differences diverse learners experience are common to *all* diverse learners, and some are specific to groups and individuals. Peer pressure is an example of one experience that occurs in all groups, including students of the dominant culture, but it also varies from group to group. Communication styles is another.

The more you know about the cultures of your diverse learners, the better equipped you will be to teach them. One of the best ways to bridge the cultural gaps to your diverse learners is to find out as much as you can about them.

Try these strategies:

**Level: Elementary/Middle/High
Subject: Cross-curricular**

- Ask students to bring in a family item and share it with the class.
- Ask a general question at the beginning of class, such as "What is your favorite food?" "What do you enjoy doing in the evenings after you finish your homework?"
- Invite parents into the school to interact with staff and students.
- Begin your year by having students write personal narratives about themselves. If you are teaching content other than English in middle or high school, you can tie this assignment to your subject matter and classroom goals. Ask students to write their "math history" or their "science history" (or whatever subject you teach) and tell you how math or science has been a part of their lives. Have them end their history with goals for your class.
- Call each student's family before the year begins and introduce yourself, expressing how excited you are to have their child in your class. Although this is time intensive, the payoff is immense.

DIVERSE LEARNERS' COMMUNICATION STYLES

Think about *your* classroom communication style. How would you describe it?

_____

_____

_____

Keep your communication style in mind as you read the following. How does your style compare to the communication styles of your diverse learners?

Communication styles differ among groups and within groups. Understanding student communication styles is critical. When we do not understand our students' cultural communication style, we may be contributing to their school failure. Some of the things that make up communication style are our nonverbal gestures and our preferences for interacting with others. Even the traditional seating arrangement of our classrooms is not necessarily the best for all students. Some cultural groups tend to learn better in groups and nontraditional seating patterns (Nieto, 1996).

Simple instructional strategies we use may conflict with some students' cultural communication styles. For example, teachers who use short "wait time" (the time a teacher gives a student to think of an answer after the teacher asks the question) can put American Indian students at a disadvantage, because their culture may teach them to think deliberately and respond more slowly after considering all options. When I teach, I call myself the Queen of Wait Time, and I count 1001, 1002, 1003, 1004, 1005, 1006, 1007 before I expect an answer from anyone. You will get a response from someone if you allow enough wait time. You could do a minilesson on answering questions, sharing with students the types of questions that require more thought and those simply needing a simple answer (of course, if you are asking many lower-level questions, you may want to examine why you are spending your time at that level).

American Indian core values emphasize respect, harmony, internal locus of control, dignity of the individual, and cooperation and sharing. A classroom that demands individualized work and competition works against these values. Cooperative learning is one strategy worth exploring with American Indian children as well as some other cultural groups such as Latino families, who also tend to focus on cooperation rather than competition (Gonzalez, Huerta-Macias, & Tinajero, 1998).

USE OF RHYTHM

Another instructional tool, the use of rhythm, may vary between the diverse learners' culture and that of the dominant teacher's culture. For example, African American adults and children may use a "contest" style of speech, based on the call-and-response patterns found in Black music (Nieto, 1996) and preaching. Teachers who are aware of this can incorporate it successfully into their lessons. You might ask students to create a study guide using a call-and-response mode and create opportunities for students who respond to this cultural mode to use their oral skills as often as possible in your classroom. They can do this through oral presentations and performances. Capitalizing upon student strengths is one of the best ways to improve achievement and reduce behavior issues.

MISREADING CULTURAL COMMUNICATION

Misreading cultural communication cues can result in behavior issues and incorrect feedback about learning. One English language learner (ELL) teacher misread the nonverbal cues of her Puerto Rican students. When they exhibited a "wrinkling of the nose," she did not know they were signifying they did not understand the material. In Alaska Native cultures, a wrinkled nose often means no and a raised eyebrow often means yes (Nieto, 1996). Not knowing the nonverbal cues of your students might cause you to assume they are acting in a disrespectful manner or not paying attention, rather than simply following your instructions. In addition, when we do not understand the communication cues of our diverse learners, we may be telling them (unintentionally) that we do not care enough about them to learn about them.

One method to learn about cultural communication cues, especially those ELLs with special education needs, is to assess students in their homes and communities. By involving parents as participants in these evaluations, educators can "minimize misdiagnoses and inappropriate special education placements" (Garcia, quoted in Artiles & Ortiz, 2002, p. 23). When the values of the educators and the parents differ, there may be cultural discomfort. If educators learn and understand the cultural, linguistic, and socioeconomic influences of their students and families, they probably will experience improved communication.

CLASSROOM BEHAVIORS

Diverse learners bring with them expectations for classroom communication with their teacher and classmates, especially how they are expected to answer questions in class. Does the student expect to give an individual answer in front of peers, use eye contact, guess an answer, or volunteer in class? These behavior expectations vary among diverse learners. Students also vary as to the amount of teacher guidance they expect (Cloud, quoted in Artiles & Ortiz, 2002). Once again, unless we make our expectations clear and model them for students, we may be placing our diverse learners in an uncomfortable classroom situation.

Time on task is another way that students often differ. How do you expect students to begin class work? Do you expect them to listen to your directions and begin immediately? Or do you take into account group styles? For example, your African American students, because they "have expressed an orientation toward collective responsibility and interdependence" (Hale-Benson, 1986, p. 16), may first interact with others, rather than immediately beginning academic work. If you are a teacher whose style is "Get to work NOW!" you may find yourself frustrated and assume that the students are attempting to avoid doing the work. Being aware of this style difference allows you to make the necessary accommodations that best fit all the students in your classroom.

African American students also tend to be multimodal (Hale-Bensen, 1986). Their involvement with classroom instruction is cognitive, emotional, and physical, all at the same time. If you are a teacher who learns cognitively, not needing the emotional and physical modes, you may have trouble understanding why some African American students may need emotional and physical connections to the material in order to learn it. On the other hand, a newly arrived Vietnamese immigrant student might feel uncomfortable in an informal classroom where students are expected to ask questions and work together.

The quiet, traditional classroom in which many of us learned, quietly seated in rows of desks and raising our hands to answer the questions the teacher posed, does not match the cultural communication styles of many of our diverse learners. What can we do?

In *Educating Latino Students,* Gonzalez, Huerta-Macias, and Tinajero (1998) suggest developing a "learning context that is multiculturally sensitive, where differences are acknowledged and appreciated and where opportunities do exist for learning in nonmainstream patterns" (p. 31). The following are aids for learning about the communication styles of our diverse learners.

- Observe your students' cultural group in your classroom, in public, and on television (some comedy sitcoms exaggerate cultural behaviors but at the same time can offer opportunities to observe cultural patterns in practice as long as we recognize they purposely stereotype characters and cultures to create humor).
- Adapt your instruction and the curriculum to meet the needs of diverse learners. Instruct using a range of different modalities and include examples from all the cultural groups in your classroom when you tell stories, use metaphors, and teach the histories of your discipline. To teach math without sharing the contributions of Africans to mathematics misses an opportunity to build cultural awareness.
- Hold meetings at school for parents to interact with and learn from them.
- Read books on body language and cultural communications.
- Hold professional workshops about diverse learners in your school.
- Ask your students.
- Ask students' parents to share their professions with a class.
- Attend conferences that include workshops on your student populations.
- Talk with educators from diverse cultural groups.
- Do home visits and observe your students with their families.

In addition to these suggested strategies, Tharp (quoted in Artiles & Ortiz, 2002) developed several guiding principles for effective pedagogy when working with ELLs with learning disabilities in general education, suggesting we work collaboratively with students; incorporate language and literacy across the curriculum, connect classroom learning to students' lives; and teach higher-level thinking through conversation (p. 140).

PEER PRESSURE

Even when we understand the communication patterns of our culturally diverse learners, we still face the effects of peer pressure, both positive and negative, in our classrooms. In "The Canary in the Mine: The Achievement Gap Between Black and White Students" (1998), Mano Singham writes of the impact of peers upon student achievement. Examining college students, Singham, using the research of John Ogbu and others, found that Chinese students often studied together and shared tips and strategies for success. African American students, on the other hand, partied together but seldom studied together. Black students often had no idea where they stood with respect to others in the class, and they were usually surprised when they received poor grades, thinking they had done exactly what was expected of them. In addition, Kunjufu (1988) examines negative peer influence on Black students who exhibit "acting White" behaviors. They may be ridiculed by their peers for buying into the dominant culture if they choose to listen in class, do their homework, and make good grades. At the runaway shelter where I taught (mentioned in Chapter 16), the young men had to hide their schoolbooks from the neighborhood gang members or risk getting beaten up or killed for "acting White." One young man related that he had to sneak down the back alley to attend the GED program for fear of his life.

Often, students lack the understanding of what it takes to make A's and B's in a rigorous academic setting. Students need to hear that in order to make A's and B's in high school, they must study hours a night, limit phone calls and television, and set up a schedule for homework. Some students are unaware of what honor roll students actually do in order to make the honor roll. Once again, there are "hidden rules" of academic achievement that must be taught to our children if we want them to achieve academically.

If you choose to change a negative peer culture at your educational site, you may want to find students who will work with you. The key to building the critical mass of students goes back to relationships. If you have a good relationship with your target students, you can begin to build a critical mass of students to focus on achievement goals. The research (Singham, 1998) presents the idea of a "critical mass" of students who need to buy into the idea of academic achievement and who, therefore, create a *positive peer culture* for achievement. Creating that critical mass in your classroom provides a supportive peer network for diverse learners. How do you do that? See the following box.

Level: Elementary/Middle/High
Subject: Cross-curricular

- Call on all students equitably.
- Ensure that your lessons include role models from the cultural groups represented in your classroom.
- Use student names in your examples.
- Impress upon students the necessity of book knowledge so they can't be cheated in their lives.
- Use cooperative learning.
- Emphasize cooperation and deemphasize competition.
- Use a "We're all in this together" classroom approach.
- Build a classroom community that expects excellence from each student and allows a flexible time frame for achieving excellence.
- Talk explicitly about the negative effects of peer pressure and how students can counteract them.
- Sponsor clubs (see Chapter 17 for a model) that support academic excellence and offer a support group to students willing to fight negative peer pressure.

The negative peer culture exists because of perceptions and belief systems; a positive peer culture can exist because of perceptions and belief systems too. You and your colleagues can find the ways that work best for you. When you put your plans into action and see the results, you will begin to see the changes in the perceptions of students as well as changes in the perceptions of the staff.

Describe the peer cultures at your educational setting.

_____

_____

_____

Devise a plan to create a critical mass of positive peer support in your classroom/in your school.

_____

_____

_____

THE STEREOTYPE THREAT

Have you ever been stereotyped? For example, if you are a woman, did others assume you could not change a tire, fix a leaky pipe, or run a business? If you are a male and an elementary teacher, did others assume that you would not be as adept at the job as the females in your building? Think about a time you were stereotyped by others.

_____

_____

_____

When you performed under this stereotype, how did it affect the outcome?

_____

_____

_____

Stereotypes are perceptions, and perceptions create our reality. Just as our cultural lens largely determines what we see and how we interpret it, our students' perceptions of themselves may affect their academic achievement. In "Thin Ice: 'Stereotype Threat' and Black College Students," Claude Steele (1999) defines the "stereotype threat" as "the threat of being viewed through the lens of a negative stereotype, or the fear of doing something that would inadvertently confirm that stereotype" (p. 46). Exploring the impact of the stereotype threat upon Black college students, Steele found that when students were presented with a difficult verbal standardized test as a test of ability, Black students performed "dramatically less well than White students," even though the groups were "matched in ability level" (p. 47). But when they presented the same test as a laboratory task that was used to study how certain problems are generally solved, the Black students' performance equaled that of the White students. Steele suggests that "race consciousness" brings about impaired achievement (p. 47).

Steele and Aronson (Steele, 1999) went on to test their hypothesis with a group of White males. They told the group that they were taking a math test on which Asians usually scored higher than Whites. The result? White males who heard this comment scored less well than the White males who did not hear this comment (p. 48).

The stereotype threat most affects the academically able students. On tests, Black students tried too hard, rereading the questions and rechecking their answers more than when they were not under the stereotype threat. Searching for solutions, Steele (1999) found that Black students who participated in discussion groups in an informal dormitory setting improved their grades and reduced their feelings of the stereotype threat. Steele suggests that we educators might spend more time in developing the trust in our schools with our African American students if we hope to see the academic achievement that our students are capable of demonstrating (p. 54).

THE "MODEL MINORITY" STEREOTYPE THREAT

Asian Americans suffer a different stereotype threat. They are often perceived as the "model minority" and depicted as diligent, quiet, intelligent, and academically able and are often seen as immigrants or foreigners, rather than minorities (Ogbu, cited in Singham, 1998). Stacey J. Lee, in *Unraveling the "Model Minority" Stereotype* (1996), finds that the stereotype silences the voices of low-achieving Asian students and denies the complexity of higher-achieving student experiences. In addition, the stereotype reinforces the "racial order by focusing on Asian American success and redirecting attention away from Whites" (p. 99). Lee argues that African American students' failure to "challenge White success is related to the silence that surrounds Whiteness in general" (p. 99). Since the model minority stereotype consists of a comparative and competitive nature, Lee found many African American students in his study who believed Asian American students were a threat. Some even believed that Asian American success was achieved at the expense of African Americans and that they were one more group who had climbed over African Americans to pursue the American dream (pp. 99–100). Moreover, Lee found a direct link between a "racial group's perceptions of their own position and their attitudes toward Asians/Asian Americans and Asian American success" (p. 121).

Interestingly, most groups of Asian-identified students blamed themselves for the challenges they faced and did not expect the dominant group to accommodate them. Of all the Asian-identified groups Lee studied, only Asian Americans challenged the dominant group. Ultimately, the model minority stereotype has been used to "support the status quo and the ideologies of meritocracy and individualism" (Lee, 1996, p. 8).

While acknowledging that being seen as a model minority carries with it a kind of privilege, Lee states that the dangers exceed the privilege. This stereotype is dangerous because of the way it has been used by the dominant group to silence Asian Americans and their experiences and against other minority groups to silence claims of inequality (Lee, 1996, p. 125). The research clearly points to the dangers of the stereotype threat experienced by some of our diverse learners.

The following are strategies to support students in combating the stereotype threat.

Level: Elementary/Middle/High
Subject: Cross-curricular

- Learn about each student as an individual.
- Do not lump students into one ethnic group. Korean students differ from Chinese students. Puerto Rican students differ from Mexican students. Immigrant children face different issues than second-generation Asian Americans or Mexican Americans. The list continues: do not assume all children of any one ethnic group are alike.
- Talk about stereotypes with your class.
- Have students share their cultural experiences.
- Do a daily check of your perceptions. Have student behaviors reinforced stereotypes? Negated them? We tend to see that which reinforces our stereotype, so we must be vigilant in doing daily perception checks.
- Include a variety of role models from the cultural groups of your students, continuing to emphasize that not all Blacks are alike, not all Whites are alike, not all Asians are alike, and so on.
- Share the literature of each of your students' cultures. The poetry, short stories, folk tales, and novels are wonderful ways to learn about cultures and to support positive dialogues.
- Encourage student forums to discuss the issues of stereotypes.
- Invite the Anti-Defamation League's World of Difference presenters to work with students and staff.
- Encourage students to write their stories and share them in a Writers' Showcase (model included later).
- Use cooperative learning to allow students to get to know each other as individuals.
- Create classroom projects that allow students to get to know each other as individuals.

This research has profound implications for our school settings. It offers a wonderful vehicle for staff discussion and problem solving. Consider using the Claude Steele (1999) article in a whole-staff discussion (you could also use this in a senior high contemporary issues class, English or history class). Encourage staff to reflect upon times when they felt a "stereotype threat." Encourage them to share this with their high school students and ask their input. Discussions about this article with groups of students might encourage an honest look at this dilemma and provide opportunities for problem solving.

Understanding the communications styles of our diverse learners and the effects of peer pressure and the stereotype threat upon them allows us to become more culturally proficient.

The following are strategies to reach diverse learners:

Level: Elementary/Middle/High
Subject: Cross-curricular

- Place value on students' home languages and cultures.
- Acquire a basic command of the language of your diverse learners. This may seem extreme, but learning to speak only a few words to your diverse learners in their native language will usually bring smiles to their faces.
- Integrate the culture, experiences, and language of diverse learners into your classroom lessons.
- Set high expectations for all diverse learners.
- Communicate these expectations to your diverse learners.
- Include professional development focusing on the cultures of your diverse learners.
- Check your instruction to see if you are following the suggestions found in *Educating Latino Students* (Gonzalez et al., 1998): Are you using a learning context that is multiculturally sensitive? Are you acknowledging and appreciating differences among your diverse learners? and Are you creating opportunities for learning in ways that differ from the mainstream?

Which suggestions in this chapter might you consider for your classroom?

_____

_____

_____

Set some goals for implementing the suggestions or strategies you found in this chapter.

_____

_____

_____

This chapter gave you some background on the challenges that diverse learners may encounter in your school setting. Chapter 3 probes more deeply into the causes of the achievement gap and offers strategies to close the gap in your classroom.

❖   ❖   ❖

SUGGESTED READING

Artiles, Alfredo J., and Alba A. Ortiz, eds. 2002. *English Language Learners With Special Education Needs.*

Gay, Geneva. 1988. *Designing Relevant Curriculum for Diverse Learners.*

Gonzalez, Maria Luisa, Ana Huerta-Macias, and Josefina Villamil Tinajero. 1998. *Educating Latino Students: A Guide to Successful Practice.*

Lee, Stacy. 1996. *Unraveling the "Model Minority" Stereotype: Listening to Asian American Youth.*

Nieto, Sonia. 1996. *Affirming Diversity: The Sociopolitical Context of Multicultural Education.*

Ogbu, John. 1991. "Immigrant and Involuntary Minorities in Comparative Perspective."

Singham, Mano. 1998. "The Canary in the Mine: The Achievement Gap Between Black and White Students."

Steele, Claude. 1999. "Thin Ice: 'Stereotype Threat' and Black College Students."

Tileston, Donna Walker. 2004. *What Every Teacher Should Know About Diverse Learners.*

3

What We Know About the Achievement Gap

Ten years ago, you probably had not heard of the "achievement gap." Yet today, talk about the achievement gap abounds in faculty meetings, educational journals, and political speeches. Standards, high-stakes testing, and disaggregated data have dropped the challenge to close the achievement gap at our school doors.

This chapter examines some of the causes for the gap and strategies to mediate the gap in a school setting. To close the gap is much more elusive. Clearly, this is a complex and complicated issue that reaches far beyond the classroom door. The achievement gap arose and continues as a result of societal issues (Noguera & Akom, 2000; Singleton & Linton, 2006; Williams, 1996).

What is the achievement gap? The achievement gap refers to the gap in academic achievement between and among student groups. Presently, the achievement gap shows large percentages of low-income African American, Latino/a, and Native American students at the low end of the achievement ladder, and large percentages of middle- and high-income White and Asian students at the top of the achievement ladder (Johnson, 2002).

Even though the gap narrowed among diverse groups in the 1970s and 1980s, this changed in the 1990s (Haycock, 2001; National Center for Education Statistics, 2000; Viadero, 2000), when the gap widened once again. The College Board's National Task Force on Minority Achievement (1999) gives us important information about the gap.

The gaps persist regardless of economic status. By second and third grades, African American, Latino/a, and Native American students are scoring lower than White or Asian students. African American, Latino/a, and Native American students score less well on standardized tests. Gaps persist in additional levels of achievement, such as grades and class rank. Gaps persist in SAT and AP scores. African American, Latino/a, and Native American students earn lower grades in college, despite similar admission test scores, and earn fewer degrees (Johnson, 2002, p. 4). In addition, African American students are more likely to be placed in special education classes, and once placed, they are less likely to be mainstreamed or returned to regular classes (Johnson, 2002).

CULTURAL EXPECTATIONS

Perhaps one explanation is as simple as the cultural expectations for academic excellence we find in our schools, for we often wear blinders that keep us from seeing the truth. Consider the following scenario:

While teaching a workshop on the gap, I suggested that the school staffs in the upper-middle-class suburban district where the workshop took place have the ability to prepare all of their students for college, notwithstanding those with severe mental disabilities. An elementary school counselor vehemently disagreed, saying, "Not all of our other kids have the ability to go to college."

I then asked the counselor the following question: "You have two children—do you expect them to go to college?"

The counselor answered, "Well, yes," in an exasperated tone.

"Then why shouldn't all your parents have the same expectations for their children?" I replied.

The next morning the counselor announced to the group that she had something to say. She told the group that she had never thought of the college question in quite the way it had been asked. She now understood that her blanket assumption that some kids don't have the ability to go to college was dangerous and potentially limiting to the students in her care, young elementary school children, ages 6 to 11, who were in their early years of academic development. The research shows that the initial labels attached to first-grade students placed in high and low groups follows them throughout their elementary and middle school careers (Johnson, 2002).

To assign an assumption to any child at any level can be dangerous. Tomlinson's work in differentiated instruction (2003) tells us that children learn in different ways and at different rates of speed. Some children need more time than others to process a learning task. Our job is to find ways to support the academic achievement of all children. In *Using Data to Close the Achievement Gap*, Ruth Johnson's (2002) research suggests that it is possible for all students to learn at grade level and it is also possible to reverse low outcomes for children that others have given up on. The counselor in the scenario above changed her belief system, moving from a belief that some groups of children were less capable than others to a belief that what she expects for her children might be what other parents expect for their children and that children may be capable of their parents' expectations. I have found this question to be a powerful one to spark discussion among staff members. It challenges our perceptions of what children can achieve.

My perceptions of what students were capable of achieving evolved over the years. Several experiences forced me to rethink my assumptions. The following three examples happened in my classrooms over time.

1. Senior high African American students with C averages were placed in the college-level composition course (in a pilot program), and they succeeded as well as White students who entered with B or A averages. Before, because of a minimum grade requirement for the college credit class, the African American students previously had not been given the chance to perform in an honors-level class.

2. Men in a maximum-security prison were placed in a college-level writing class (most with only a GED certificate, not a high school diploma), and on the whole, they performed as well as or better than the college students I taught on the university campus.

3. Students who did not perform well in a seventh-grade English class matriculated into honors English during their sophomore or junior years in high school. Because I taught these students both in middle school and as freshmen in high school, I witnessed their cognitive growth as they evolved into honor students. They matured cognitively at a slower rate than other students placed in freshman honors English. However, had they been judged by their seventh-grade English performance and retained in the average track, their potential to do the honors work would have been overlooked.

These three examples illustrate that learners develop cognitively at different rates and are capable of doing higher-level work.

Think about a time when someone in your life did not have high expectations for you. How did you feel? What did you do?

_____

_____

_____

Think about a time when your students outperformed your expectations for them.

_____

_____

_____

How did that affect future expectations for your students?

_____

_____

_____

Recently, an educator shared that although she came from a family where no one had previously attended college, she was placed in a high school where nearly everyone attended college. Because her peers assumed that they and she would be attending college, she assumed that she would be attending college. She now holds a college degree and is a teacher. But, she added, had she been in a school where the "school culture" did not support attending college, she might have accepted her family's past and made no attempt to attain a college degree.

- The school culture determines, in part, the academic achievement of its students.
- Our perceptions (our cultural lens) determine, in part, the academic achievement of our students.

If we want to raise the academic achievement of all students in our schools, we must address the school culture and the personal lens through which we view our students. We have to ask ourselves the hard question: Do we expect to find an achievement gap? If so, why? Researchers suggest myriad reasons; however, the following five offer us opportunities for mediation and change. They are poverty, academic course work, test bias, teacher expectations, and teacher quality.

POVERTY

How does poverty contribute to the achievement gap?

One in five children lives in poverty in the United States, more than most industrialized Western countries (Brooks-Gunn et al., quoted in Marzano, 2004). Poverty contributes to lower test scores, psychological stresses, and lack of language acquisition. In addition, poverty and ethnicity are linked. The U.S. Census Bureau (cited in Marzano, 2004, p. 11) shows that 32.9 million people, or 11.7%, in the United States live below the poverty line. About 12 out of every 100 people live in poverty; however, for Hispanics and African Americans, it is higher. Approximately 22.7% of African Americans and 21.4% of Hispanics live at or below the poverty line; for White people, it is 9.9% (Marzano, 2004). If children are born African American or Hispanic, they have more than twice the chance of being born into poverty.

In _Using Data to Close the Achievement Gap_, Ruth Johnson (2002) states that we must kill the myth that children living in poverty and some racial/ethnic groups are "incapable of anything but low outcomes" (p. 11). In fact, Marzano's research, cited in _Building Background Knowledge for Academic Achievement_

(Marzano, 2004), indicates that "innate intelligence is not as strongly related to academic achievement as once thought" and "learned intelligence is the stronger correlate of success in school" (p. 13). Therefore, if the knowledge and skill that affluent students bring with them into the classroom is learned rather than innate, then students from poverty can learn it too (p. 14).

The anecdote about the counselor demonstrates the myth that well-meaning educators can carry with them. Only by exposing this myth can we create the academic culture all children deserve.

There is little doubt that poverty plays a role in the achievement gap, yet many educators are aware of data that prove otherwise. In fact, Johnson (2002) finds tremendous resistance to using the data that prove poor children can achieve. She calls this unwillingness to use the data a "conspiracy of silence." However, when districts use this data with caring educators, it is possible to develop a belief that "all children are capable of achieving at academic levels for enrollment in baccalaureate degree-granting institutions" (p. xvii).

The 1999 U.S. census data (cited in Marzano, 2004) indicate that 33% of African American children live in poverty. Even though this is abominably high, we have to remember that the majority of African American children *do not* live in poverty. Yet some educators assume that because a child is Black, he or she must be poor. Many educators equate poverty with lower academic achievement.

It is true that the majority of "schools of poverty" have lower standardized test scores than the majority of schools with an affluent population. Also, fewer students attending schools of poverty attend college; however, having students in your classroom who live in families with low yearly incomes does not automatically mean that these students will not or cannot achieve. There are many additional reasons to consider when examining low student achievement. If you encounter educators who blame low academic achievement solely on poverty, suggest that they check the SAT test scores, which show that poor Whites outperform the most affluent African American students (Singleton & Linton, 2006). This fact alone indicates that other reasons in addition to poverty cause the academic achievement gap between African American students and White students.

One reason, of course, is that in schools of poverty, there are usually fewer resources than exist in schools of affluence. Having worked in schools where 98% of the students are on reduced lunch, the disparities between these schools' resources and those of the schools in affluent districts are obvious. Some of these disparities exist in the "things" available to both students and staff; some exist in the expectations of both students and staff.

Can you and your school actually address the poverty of your students' families? There are school staffs who do this in creative ways. In one school the principal bought a washer/dryer and allowed parents to clean their clothes at the school if they volunteered while their clothes were being washed and dried. If you consider that a parent may be spending more than $100 monthly at a laundromat after paying for the soap, machines, and transportation, this could be a tremendous savings for a family. It also maintains the dignity of the parent.

Other schools provide rooms where children can be fitted for shoes and clothes. And still other schools provide free computer instruction for parents, parent rooms with resources, and so on. So there are ways that schools can mediate poverty while maintaining the dignity of all involved.

Think about the times when you needed money. What kinds of stress did that give you? Were you more irritable? Did you make more mistakes than usual?

_____

_____

_____

Imagine what it must feel like to be parents who cannot provide adequately for their children. What things can you do to provide support with dignity for your students living in poverty?

_____

_____

_____

One thing we educators can do—and it is free but not easy—is to examine our assumptions about students living in poverty. When I did that, I was shocked and ashamed of what I found. I grew up in a church where we often collected money for the "poor," and I learned to pity "poor" people. These teachings seeped into my classroom instruction. For many years, my unexamined assumptions were a trap that possibly led to inequitable instruction and lowered expectations for students living in poverty.

We must consciously fight against stereotyping students as "poor" students, feeling sorry for them, and lowering expectations for them. All students need to be held to high standards. At the same time, we know different children have different needs. One child may have a learning disability and another child may be living in poverty, but that does not mean that either deserves pity. Instead, it is our responsibility as educators to provide a rigorous curriculum along with the scaffolding each child needs to achieve at high levels.

If you want to understand the impact of generational poverty upon student behaviors and achievement, examine the schools of high poverty that are closing the achievement gap. These schools do exist. There are poor schools in Harlem as well as in other urban and rural areas throughout the United States that are closing the gap. These are schools that have examined their school culture, improved teacher quality and expectations, provided additional resources for students, and addressed the needs of their specific populations. After examining schools of poverty where children academically achieve at high levels, we must conclude that "perhaps it isn't poverty, or racial/ethnic background in and of itself, but rather our response to it" (Johnson, 2002, p. 6).

ACADEMIC COURSE WORK

Rigorous academic course work makes a difference, and studies show that compared to Whites, a disproportionately small number of African American, Latino/a, and Native American students take challenging courses. Some schools rigidly track (group students according to ability), and by high school, students in the lower track may have no possibility of taking an academically challenging class (Johnson, 2002). Some minority students opt out of academically challenging courses because of peer pressure; some students do not want to do the work. Some urban schools do not offer calculus or advanced physics or chemistry.

Some educators, sadly, steer African American students away from academically challenging courses, thinking that the students need to take more "practical" classes or classes in which they will not fail. African American educators continue to relate personal stories of how high school educators told them they did not "need" to go to college or they would not be able to succeed in college. This problem still occurs.

What can schools do to encourage African American, Latino/a, and Native American students to take academically challenging courses? Try the following strategies:

- Take whatever steps are necessary to ensure that each child reads at grade level.
- Offer students positive role models. Post throughout the school posters of minority engineers, scientists, writers, doctors, judges, and so on. How many steps do you have to take inside your school before you see a picture or poster of role models in a profession other than sports who reflect the ethnicity of your students?
- Hire minority staff.
- Begin "college talk" on Day 1. Assume each child will attend college.
- Carefully monitor students as they progress through elementary school. Notice their strengths. Inquire about their dreams. Encourage their dreams.
- Begin to offer specialized clubs at upper elementary school level, such as science club, math club, chess club, foreign language clubs, writers' club, and academic club. Ensure that diverse learners are central participants in these clubs.
- Take students to visit local universities in middle school, if not before.
- Call your students "scholars" (Kunjufu, 1988) when you address them in class.
- Identify local university students who will mentor middle school students.
- Ensure that each high school student has a mentor who encourages him or her to take a rigorous academic course of study.
- Find teachers who really want diverse learner students in their advanced classes and who will support their success.
- Organize a Student Support Club (see Chapter 17 for one model) so that the students will have positive peer support.

What can you do in your own classroom or school to ensure that diverse learners enroll in your most academically rigorous courses?

_____

_____

_____

How can you shape your instructional practices to ensure that you offer the most academically rigorous work to all students?

_____

_____

_____

Grant Wiggins and Jay McTighe (1998) offer educators an invaluable framework for teacher planning in their book *Understanding by Design*. Based on standards, this book presents a lesson plan design. This lesson plan design is a model of "backward design" that begins with the desired results, proceeds to the acceptable evidence of those results, and ends with the learning experiences and instruction that guarantee those results.

After completing a workshop using *Understanding by Design*, an art teacher commented that she now understands how learning fits together. She explained that before her experience with this design framework, she had students complete one art project after another, never thinking through why they were doing them and how and what learning resulted. Now she designs lessons for understanding based on the results she wants from her students. She remarked that it has not only changed her instructional practice, but it has also created a new excitement in her classroom because now her entire school year provides a rich, cohesive educational experience.

Using *Understanding by Design,* or a similar lesson design book, will enrich your planning experience and increase the academic achievement of your students.

TEST BIAS

Test bias is a complex issue. Many researchers now say that test bias has been largely eliminated. Much has been eliminated, but often bias remains because of the cultures in which we live. Even though test makers scrutinize tests, the playing field is far from level.

Teachers have shared personal anecdotes about their students and the tests. Some students are tested over things they have not experienced in their lives. One teacher said a recent test had a passage about grasshoppers, but her students did not know what grasshoppers were. In addition, particular words can hold different meanings for different children, such as the word *weave,* which may mean a kind of stitchery to one child and a hairpiece to another.

Studying the language of test taking is relevant for educators. If we want all of our children to close the academic achievement gap, we must teach all children the language of test taking. If children lack knowledge of the language of test taking, they may be unable to interpret the test language.

To eliminate further test bias, do the following:

- Get involved in the test-making process in your state.
- Write test items for the ACT.
- Teach students to read critically.
- Use a wide variety of reading materials to build background knowledge.
- Select old test items to use as opening activities in class. Do one a day for practice.
- Teach your students the concept that language gives them power, and give them numerous examples of how language empowers their lives. Tell them that they must learn standard English in order to succeed in college.
- Work with your entire staff to determine areas of concern on state tests.
- Have your students create test passages and items.
- Teach your students the art of test taking.
- Brainstorm with your students ways to create a positive test experience.
- Do everything you can do to make the test-taking experience a positive one—several books in the marketplace give you numerous strategies to address test taking.
- Look upon the testing situation as an opportunity rather than a negative experience for you and your students.
- Use test data to improve your instruction.

Are you a good test taker? Why, or why not?

_____

_____

_____

What things can you do to improve the test-taking abilities of all of your students?

_____

_____

_____

In what ways can you use standardized test data to improve your instructional practice?

_____

_____

_____

TEACHER EXPECTATIONS

In her book _The Dreamkeepers: Successful Teachers of African American Students_, Gloria Ladson-Billings (1994) states that successful teachers treat students as competent, use a _no-deficit_ model, provide instructional "scaffolding," focus on instruction with a sacrosanct reading period, extend students' thinking and abilities, and possess in depth knowledge of both subject matter and the students (pp. 123–125).

What are teacher expectations?

_____

_____

_____

In the learning process, teacher expectations include teacher engagement. In Chapter 7 of _Closing the Achievement Gap_, "Teacher Engagement and Real Reform in Urban Schools," Karen Louis and BetsAnn Smith (cited in Williams, 1996) write about teacher engagement as integral to teacher expectations. Students must believe their teachers are engaged with the content and care about them as individuals. Unless this occurs, students fail to engage with the content. Teachers must believe that their students are engaged with the content. Unless this occurs, teachers do not teach at optimal levels of instruction. This creates a catch-22 (p. 125).

This catch-22 appears to be especially true for schools with a high concentration of lower income and minority students. Compared with teachers of more affluent children, teachers who work with students from poorer families are more likely to believe that they have little influence on their students' learning.

Think about your "teacher engagement." How engaged are you?

_____

_____

_____

What influences your teacher engagement?

_____

_____

_____

What can you do to ensure that you remain engaged throughout the school year?

_____

_____

_____

Write out your expectations of your students. Do they vary, depending upon which students you consider?

_____

_____

_____

Do you truly believe that your diverse learners can achieve at the same levels as White males? What proof do you have that you believe this?

_____

_____

_____

What concrete steps can you take to ensure that your teacher expectations are high enough for all of your students?

_____

_____

_____

How do you find out what your students are capable of achieving? Try the following:

- Examine your state tests. They offer one standard of judgment.
- Visit a school, public or private, that graduates students who have achieved academically at top levels. Examine the curriculum and student work.
- Examine student work with your colleagues at your school setting, using a "critical friends" model or some other model for discussion.
- Read award-winning student literary magazines and newspapers.
- Attend science fairs and view winning projects.
- Attend conferences to network with educators and participate in sessions.
- Examine your subconscious prejudices and perceptions.

A book that clearly demonstrates how teacher expectations create a classroom of excellence is Erin Gruwell's (1999) _The Freedom Writers Diary: How a Teacher and 150 Teens Used Writing to Change Themselves and the World Around Them._

TEACHER QUALITY

What does teacher quality mean to you?

_____

_____

_____

For the past several years, Kati Haycock (2001) has researched teacher quality. In searching for the causes of the achievement gap, she and her research colleagues ask adults why there is a gap. They hear comments from educators that the children are too poor, the parents don't care, and they come to school hungry. The reasons, she adds, are always about the children and their families. Yet, when she talks with students, she hears different reasons. Students talk about teachers who do not know their subject matter, counselors who underestimate their potential and misplace them, administrators who dismiss their concerns, and a curriculum and expectations that are so low level that students are bored (p. 7).

Haycock (2001) agrees that poverty and parental education matter, but she states that we take the children who have the least and "give them less of everything that we believe makes a difference" (p. 8). High school students who take more rigorous course work learn more and perform better on tests (Haycock, 2001; Johnson, 2003). The more rigorous the courses students take, the better they perform. Also, the rigor and quality of high school course work determines success in college. By giving the honors work to all children, we create exciting, rigorous classrooms set for achievement.

Haycock's (2001), Johnson's (2002), and others' research show that all students can achieve at high levels if they are taught at high levels. Recent research has turned _upside down_ the assumptions previously made about why students did not achieve. Those assumptions were the belief that "what students learned was largely a factor of their family income or parental education, not of what schools did" (Haycock, 2001, p. 10). We now know that what schools do matters and that what teachers do may matter most of all.

Do you agree or disagree with Kati Haycock's findings?

_____

_____

_____

Describe your teacher quality.

_____

_____

_____

In what ways might you improve your teacher quality? Design a plan for yourself.

_____

_____

_____

This chapter covered ways that poverty, test bias, academic course work, teacher expectations, and teacher quality impact the achievement gap. The strategies listed in this chapter have been implemented in schools at every level. Consider the strategies and choose some that you believe will work for you. You may also consider working with your colleagues in a professional learning community in your school to examine the gap and ways to mediate and close the gap in your district. In Chapter 4, you are presented with a list of questions to consider about your professional experiences. These questions can be used as self-reflective tools, journal prompts, and discussion starters. They are yours to keep, think about, use, and add to as we continue our inquiry into classroom instruction and how to support the academic success of diverse learners.

❖   ❖   ❖

SUGGESTED READING

Calkins, Lucy, et al. 1998. *A Teacher's Guide to Standardized Reading Tests: Knowledge Is Power.*

Ehrenreich, Barbara. 2001. *Nickel and Dimed: On (Not) Getting By in America.*

Haberman, Martin. 1995. *STAR Teachers of Children in Poverty.*

Haycock, Kati. 2001. Closing the Achievement Gap. *Educational Leadership* (March), 6–11.

Johnson, Ruth S. 2002. *Using Data to Close the Achievement Gap.*

Ladson-Billings, Gloria. 1994. *The Dreamkeepers: Successful Teachers of African American Children.*

Wiggins, Grant, and Jay McTighe. 1998. *Understanding by Design.*

Williams, Belinda. 1996. *Closing the Achievement Gap: A Vision for Changing Beliefs and Practices.*

PART II

Examining
Our Inner World

4

Reflecting on the Educator Self

The previous two chapters focused on your students. In this chapter, you are invited to think about the important questions in *your* life. Which questions deepen your understanding of your profession? In *The Courage to Teach: Exploring the Inner Landscape of a Teacher's Life*, Parker Palmer (1998) asks this question: "How can the teacher's selfhood become a legitimate topic in education and in our public dialogues on educational reform?" (p. 3). Our selfhoods must become legitimate dialogue if we wish to reach across cultures and support the academic excellence of our diverse learners. As Palmer says, "As long as we inhabit a universe made homogeneous by our refusal to admit otherness, we can maintain the illusion that we possess the truth about ourselves and the world—after all, there is no 'other' to challenge us!" (p. 38). However, when we open ourselves to the "other" and admit that they (the other) may have different life experiences and perspectives, the "truths we have built our lives on begin to feel fragile" (p. 38). Ultimately, the more we know about ourselves, the better we can reach and support our diverse learners.

REFLECTIVE QUESTIONS

What questions do you ask yourself as you reflect on your work? The following questions offer you an opportunity to reflect on simple things that make a difference in working with diverse learners: your heart, your body, and your interactions with students and colleagues. These questions address the who of your teaching, a piece that is just as necessary, if not more so, than the what, how, and why.

- Do my students leave my classroom at the end of the school year liking more the subject I teach them than when they entered? For example, an English teacher would ask, "Do my students like to read and write more in June than they did in September?"

_____

_____

_____

- What does my body language say to my students? Do I lean into some children but lean away from others when I communicate with them? Is there incongruity between my body language and my spoken words? Do I understand the body language and social cues of each of the cultures represented in my classes?

_____

_____

_____

- Do my interactions with my colleagues model the kinds of interactions I expect among my students? And if not, how can I change my interactions with colleagues?

_____

_____

_____

- Do my interactions with my students model the kinds of behaviors I expect back from them? If I scream at them to sit down or scowl at them, can I expect to see the same behaviors mirrored back to me?

_____

_____

_____

- Do I know about the cultures of my students? If I were going to teach in France, I would learn about French customs/language, and so on, yet I may be teaching children from Bosnia and know nothing about their culture.

_____

_____

_____

- Do my school environment and my classroom reflect the kinds of achievement I expect from my students? Do I post images of diverse role models, in addition to sports and entertainment figures, clearly in view for my students? What are the subconscious and hidden messages we send students when they do not see people who look like them portrayed in their place of learning? Try this at your school. How many steps must you walk into your school before you see a picture posted of a culturally diverse person? Does it matter? A local university has an office where more than 10 White men's pictures hang on the wall with no pictures of women or culturally diverse individuals. The assistant in the office, a culturally diverse middle-aged woman, shared how working under their stares each day saps her energy. Ask yourself this question again, after you read the story of Dorothy, an educator and administrator, in the next two chapters: Does it matter?

_____

_____

_____

- Do I love my subject content? Am I a voracious reader? Do I regularly cut out articles from journals, newspapers, and magazines about my subject matter to share with my students?

_____

_____

_____

- Do I have a deep and broad understanding of my subject content? Do I make my subject matter explicit? Do I talk about how I learn and what I must do to learn?

_____

_____

_____

• Do I use an educational design such as *Understanding by Design* by Grant Wiggins and Jay McTighe (1998) when I prepare my lesson plans? Do I use research-based instructional strategies such as those found in Sousa's (2001) or Marzano's (1997, 2001, 2003, 2004) works?

_____

_____

_____

• Do I practice my subject content? If I teach literacy or English, am I a writer and reader? If I teach physical education, do I keep myself physically healthy and fit? Students pay attention to what I *do*, not what I say, so do I practice what I preach?

_____

_____

_____

• Do I take care of myself? Do I eat healthily, exercise, care for my mental, physical, and spiritual self? And if I don't, how can I expect to be the best teacher I can be for my students?

_____

_____

_____

Consider using the above prompts for your personal/professional journal. You may want to select one a week to address in your journal as you journey through your school year. You may want to begin your department meetings with one set of questions and discuss them in the group for the first 15 minutes of the meeting. You may want to use these at the onset of each book study meeting in your professional learning community. Using these prompts, you may find common ground with colleagues as you work together to examine your inner worlds.

In the next two chapters, you will not only examine the inner world of Dorothy but also of Bonnie, another educator and author of this book. They share their racial history and daily lives. Chapters 5 and 6 continue to set the stage, while subsequent chapters take place in the classroom, giving you strategies to support the academic achievement of diverse learners. As you gaze into the minds of these two educators in the next two chapters, think about your colleagues who teach in the rooms next to yours. Are they so different?

5

Exploring Our Racial Identity

In this chapter, we explore our racial identity. In order to understand ourselves more deeply and, I submit, to bridge better the cultural gap between the diverse learner and ourselves (if you are a White teacher), we must explore our racial identity. When we read the racial histories of others and share our own in writing or conversation, we expose ourselves. As we share with others who do not look like us, we learn that their experiences, though similar in many ways, also differ in many ways. This chapter offers us the opportunity to reflect on the impact of one's history upon student achievement.

We live in a racialized society, and race impacts us 100% of the time, no matter our color (Singleton & Linton, 2006). One way to understand better how race impacts us is to write our racial histories and share and compare them with others, especially those who differ from ourselves. The following two racial histories are examples; however, in no way are these representative of whole groups or cultures. Instead, they are the individual histories of two educators, one who is the author of this book and one who is her close friend. By sharing our histories with each other, we learned more about how our past experiences often dictate our motivations, reactions to incidents, and the decisions we make in our daily lives. We also found that our histories sparked conversations between us about the impact of race in our lives.

The first is my racial history. I concentrate on events in my life that deal specifically with racial issues. The second is Dorothy's racial history. We have been close friends since 1983, but it was not until I read her racial history that I learned of many of the childhood (and, I might add, horrific) incidents she experienced that I was spared simply because I am White. Our skin color barely differs, since I am an olive-skinned White person and she is a light-skinned

African American person. Yet in this racialized society in which we live, our life experiences have differed greatly and continue to differ today (as you will read in the next chapter) simply because she is Black and I am White.

The prompts following our racial histories offer you an opportunity to examine your own racial identity. By exploring our racial identity and personal experiences related to race, perhaps we can understand better the challenges of race our diverse learners of color confront in their lives.

My story may be typical of other small-town White women who experienced childhood in the 1950s, went to college in the 1960s, and began teaching during a time of great unrest in our country. These women may have been active in the civil rights movement or the women's movement, or perhaps they were spectators to these events, yet deeply involved with teaching the children who would enter this changing world. It was not until the 1980s that I began to realize how these prior years shaped my thinking and my need to understand the world from more than the myopic lens of my past. In no way do I believe that I understand all perspectives; in fact, the more I learn, the more I understand that the "I don't know what I don't know" continues to expand rather than diminish in my life.

MY STORY

Childhood

I was born a White female in 1946 to middle-class parents in a small town set on the Mississippi River. No one on either side of my family had attended college, but after I was born, my father, a decorated veteran of World War II, entered and graduated from a small state college, using the GI Bill of Rights to pay his tuition. I attended Roman Catholic schools, K–12, and my role models were the nuns who taught us.

My family did not own a television set until I was an adolescent, and I grew up in a White world, so White that I did not realize that the record albums I purchased were sung by Black people. I assumed that because I saw no visual evidence to the contrary (sometimes album covers purposely did not display pictures of the performers if they were Black), groups such as the Coasters and the Shirelles were White people. As a child, I remember knowing no Jewish people, no Hispanic people, no Asian people, and only one Black man who drove the school bus to the convent that housed my kindergarten class. My young world was divided into the cultural groups of Catholics and non-Catholics.

Adolescence

When I was in eighth grade, a Black male joined our class during the basketball season. One night after a victory, the coach took the team and the class supporters to the Southern Café. When they would not serve our star player, the coach stood up and marched us out the door. This experience was my first known encounter with discrimination.

Adulthood

During college I married my first husband, and while planning our wedding, I observed racial discrimination for the second time. I had made friends with a Black girl from St. Louis and wanted to invite her to my wedding. My mother objected, saying my grandmother would not enter the church with a Negro inside. This was my first awareness of discrimination in my family, since I had never heard my parents make a negative comment about race. When I shared my mother's comment with the priest who was to marry me, he told me to invite her because that was the Christian thing to do. I did, but she did not attend.

Soon I entered graduate school at the University of Mississippi in Oxford, Mississippi. There I mixed with many Blacks on the streets, and even now I remember the signs at the ice cream drive-in that said "Colored only" and the two separate waiting rooms at the dentist's office, one carpeted with nice chairs for the Whites, the other bare floored with beat-up furniture for the Blacks. Even though Black students were allowed to register for classes in 1967, I did not have a single Black person in any of my graduate classes over the period of five summers. I did begin to notice that the ground crews at the university consisted mostly of Black men, and the foremen were mostly White. Also, I observed firsthand the humiliation that Black women suffered daily when they were asked to step behind a White woman in line at the grocery store. Even though this happened to me, as a 21-year-old young woman, I did nothing more than say, occasionally, "It's okay, you can go ahead. I'm not in a hurry."

However, I became increasingly interested in the inequities I witnessed in our society. My graduate study focused on the works of William Faulkner, and even though I followed both his fiction and his life journey as it related to race, I could not articulate clearly what was growing in my mind. Yet I had found an author who spoke to my soul and carried me to a place in America's literary world that delineated the crux of racism and our collective unconscious.

In 1967, I entered teaching and taught in a junior high school in the suburbs of St. Louis. The school was all White, and the haves and the have nots consisted of those who lived a middle-class existence and those who eked out an existence on the banks of the small river that ran through the area. They were referred to by some staff and students as the "river rats."

I lived in the White suburbs of St. Louis for the next several years, returning to Ole Miss each summer. My daughter was born in Oxford, Mississippi, the same week that the first man walked on the moon. She entered her parents' world where our church was White, our schools were White, our neighborhoods were White, and our lives were White.

Another Culture

It was not until after a divorce in 1975 that I entered another world. On my 30th birthday, I met the man who would become my second husband. When I wrote my mother that I was dating a man and, "by the way, he is Black," she wrote me a letter telling me I had ruined my father's 56th birthday with this news. She accused me of seeing him as a payback for their not letting me invite my Black girlfriend to my first wedding 10 years earlier.

Perhaps naively, I was shocked at my parents' response. I really hadn't thought that they were prejudiced. By this time, my grandmother had died, and I thought their reservation had disappeared with her death. I married my second husband in secret, and he was not welcome in my parents' house until after the birth of our son. I faced, with the birth of my son, experiences I would have never known in my all-White world. In the hospital, the nurse marked "Caucasian" on my son's hospital information without asking. Weeks later, as I changed his diaper in a department store bathroom, a Black woman noticed the black and blue spot at the base of his spine, and like a fortune-teller foretelling his future, she whispered ominously, "He must be biracial because he has the 'mark.'" The mark disappeared, kinky hair replaced my son's straight birth hair, and his skin darkened as he grew. I was now the mother of a biracial child in my White world.

The Voluntary Desegregation Program

In 1984 the St. Louis Voluntary Desegregation Program brought Black children to the school where I taught, a suburban high school that had previously held only White students. Partway through the year, a science teacher brought a girl to me and asked if I would proofread a letter she had written to the school board.

I read her letter and wept. She wrote that the Black children bused daily to our high school were largely ignored—invisible. The words of novelist Ralph Ellison (1952), author of *Invisible Man*, echoed in my head as I thought about the cloak of invisibility African Americans often experience in our society.

After reading the letter, I knew we had to do something at our school to support our Black students. We started a multicultural club, the Organization for the Appreciation of Black Culture, and invited all students and teachers to join. For the next five years, this club offered the "transfer" students, as they were often called, a place to discuss issues and network with others.

My Journey Continues

I began to study in earnest a world that I didn't know I didn't know. Luckily, I found mentors, Blacks and Whites, who gave me books to read, offered me opportunities, such as studying with James Banks in Seattle, and traveling to Africa to study the impact of African literature upon African American literature. Traveling to Africa, I found yet another world.

The next decade brought professional change as I completed a PhD in English, focusing on the impact of race and gender in the literary canon; moved from teaching to professional development; changed districts; and eventually accepted a position with a local service center at the University of Missouri. For the past five years, I have had the good fortune to work in several inner-city schools at the elementary, middle, and high school levels. In these schools, I have had the opportunity to work with teachers and students and continue my personal and professional journey.

My children grew to adulthood, forever impacted by the effects of racism in our society, yet often protected from its insidiousness by their family and our middle-class stature. Their stories must come from them.

For 20 years, I have read and studied racism, yet I continue to make mistakes, take my White privilege for granted, and do the "White talk" Alice McIntyre (1997) refers to in *Making Meaning of Whiteness: Exploring Racial Identity With White Teachers* even when it limits others' opportunities. This journey is lifelong; however, I am fortunate to have allies along the way.

One of these is my close friend, Dorothy Kelly. In the mid-1980s we became close friends, and she continues to provide me an alternate lens to see the world.

DOROTHY'S STORY

Childhood

I was born in 1957 in a small town in mid-Missouri. I attended public schools, K–12, and most of my role models before adolescence were older people. I lived in a rural African American community, so I can be classified as what some African Americans call "country." I lived there with my paternal grandparents during my early childhood. After leaving the "country," I lived with my maternal grandmother and spent most of my childhood between two mid-Missouri towns. Although segregation was the law in my early years, by virtue of the size of both towns, we always lived in close proximity to White people. As a child I knew and understood that White people were in charge of everything outside of my home, but I was also taught that White people were not better than Black people.

My first lesson in understanding what being an African American meant was taught by my grandmother. She drove to the poor White section of town to show me impoverished White people, and she told me not to be ashamed of being a Negro, because White people had a hard time in this world too. She told me that no one was any better than anyone else, but you had to work hard in school because some White people would keep Negroes from making a good living. I learned most of life's lessons from my grandmother.

Outside of my home life, I was encouraged by other strong Black women and men to be an independent thinker. My neighbor across the street, who was the secretary of our local NAACP and one of my friends' mother, used to send me and her daughter to the local Rexall drugstore every Saturday to sit at the counter to order milk shakes or cherry sodas. At that time I didn't know that we were being sent there as an act of civil disobedience. We were instructed to sit there until we were served and report back everything that was said to or about us. Luckily, we were served with no incidents. This was in the mid-1960s when I was in first through third grades.

One of the more fun times of my childhood was playing softball. One of the White community members started a girls' softball team. Everyone, Black and White, thought he was very brave, because he recruited mostly Black girls to play on his team. A few White girls joined, but the majority of the players were Black. We ranged in age from 10 to 16 years old. Our club sponsor was the local Dairy Queen. We traveled to small local towns and communities to play, and we won most of our games. Sometimes we could not play in the towns after dark or had to leave right after the game ended. Rarely were we allowed to even get drinks at the water fountains. Sometimes we would purposely go to the fountains when the coach told us that we were not allowed. One summer we won the league championship. We had been warned that we would be run out of town if we won. As soon as the game was over, we got out of town. It was a very scary and fun time for us, and we laughed about the situation, but the older girls were ready to fight if we had to defend ourselves. Interestingly, our parents did not go to the out-of-town games; it was just us and the coach. He was the bravest White man of my childhood.

My elementary school officially integrated—that is so much the wrong word—officially desegregated when I was in the fifth grade. We had to walk across town to a school that housed the fifth and sixth grades from the entire town in order to comply with the 1954 *Brown v. Board of Education* ruling. The local high school had been desegregated since the early 1960s. When we walked through the White neighborhoods, all the White residents came out and stood along the roads as the Black kids walked to the newly "integrated" school. We were scared and embarrassed because they thought we were going to do something to them or their property. Eventually, they stopped coming out, and we were walking to and from school without incident.

My first real understanding of being racially desegregated came at this school. I had been with most of these students in one classroom for five years; we simply moved together to the next grade. But now my class was separated. We had never known that kind of separation, but it was very clear where you stood in society after the implementation of court-ordered integration.

I still have flashbacks of racially charged incidents during my childhood. Racial slurs and being banned from playing with White students was pretty much everyday activity. There were times of civic unrest when a Black girl was selected homecoming queen or band majorette, and the Black community members were worried about violence at the high school because, invariably, the White students and parents would become angry. I also remember when one of those young ladies was the first Black hired by a local financial company as a clerk. The local NAACP and a united group of church elders had many meetings before those kinds of employment decisions were finalized. There were many "first" Blacks, and there was always backlash from the hiring or selection of that first Black.

Adolescence

As I entered junior high, I encountered what it was like to be the "first one" or the "only one." My junior high years spanned Grades 7–9. I was the first African American cheerleader at my junior high school. Because the Black girls knew there would be only one Black chosen, the predicament made us act mean toward one another. After being selected, I was very excited and happy, but that soon ended, and the reality of being the first Black cheerleader at my junior high consumed me. It was extremely odd always being on the outside of the White cheerleader clique. When we were making decisions about uniforms, hairstyles, or cheering stunts, they would whisper among themselves to agree on who would try to explain to me how to be a cheerleader. I felt odd and they felt odd. I was almost relieved when I became ill and had to have surgery and couldn't be a cheerleader. Once again, I was on the outside looking in as the rest of the Black girls again became competitive and divisive as they vied for that one spot. Some girls argued over who would be the best person to take my place, while others made bets on who might get selected even though they were not good at cheering. Some of the White parents and their daughters became outraged because only Black girls could try out as my replacement—that's desegregation. I was glad to be through with the whole mess.

In my second year in junior high, I was the first Black student council member, which was an exciting time for me because I felt like I was able to make a difference and I wasn't selected because of my race. I got to see the kids in my social studies class hold their hands up, both Black and White, and I knew I was legitimately voted in because the kids wanted me.

I felt a sense of independence; it was a racially uplifting time—my early adolescence. But as I entered my high school years, I moved to a neighboring larger university town. Although I knew my relatives who lived there, this town presented my midadolescence with a host of new friends, and acceptance was tenuous. Perhaps because I was considered a nice, friendly young lady and easy to talk to, I made friends with White students. Along with these friendships came a price. The price was being exposed to their racial history. I had a really cool White girlfriend, who had a Volkswagen, and we would hang out together. One day we were getting into her car and a good White friend of mine made this remark, "I don't ride nigger." (This was a local expression sometimes voiced by a White person who did not want to ride in the back seat.) She immediately apologized. I told her I don't consider myself to be a nigger. We got through it, and we are still friends. Once, with another group of friends at a park, we observed a Black family having a reunion. A girl in our group burst out laughing and said, "Hey, there's a coon reunion!" Whenever I heard "nigger" or "coon," I didn't hesitate to remind my White friends that I didn't put up with that talk and they shouldn't use it around me.

One of my high school sweethearts was a White guy, and he found himself often berated and called "nigger lover" by some of the White boys. My boyfriend lost some White friends along the way, and he also kicked butts because he would get so upset at racism. However, just like many other adolescents in the 1970s, we saw ourselves as righting the world and being together because we wanted to be together, not because we were a Black and White couple. We selected our friends on how they treated us, not because of race.

I still resent how I was treated by my high school counselor—I believe that to him I really did not matter. Prior to leaving high school, everyone met the high school counselor, whom we looked to for guidance on how to go to college. It never occurred to me that I wouldn't go to college. I was excluded from the Upward Bound program that most Black students participated in at my high school. The program was designed to acclimate Black high school juniors and seniors to college life. I still don't know why I was excluded from the program other than the fact that we did not receive social aid from the government or live in government housing.

My guidance counselor did not give me any encouragement, ideas, or suggestions about going to college. So, as a result, I had no idea that you could get financial aid, what college would cost, or how one got into college. I walked to the local university and found the office of admissions. The receptionist told me what

I had to do in order to get into college. By the end of my summer, I had taken and passed the ACT, then began classes in the fall. Without any guidance, I selected the wrong classes and did not have a good experience in my freshman year.

Adulthood

As I entered college in the late 1970s, my world expanded to encounter other people of color from all over the world. I had come to experience the world from a multicultural perspective. I spent a lot of time with foreign students and learned about their lives and how they were impacted by race and racism. I majored in history and eventually decided to become a teacher because I wanted all students to feel that they were special. I believed that I could help my students to understand the world and accept others and not practice prejudice, discrimination, or racism. I also believed that their understanding of the world would come from learning about everyone's history. It wasn't until my early 30s that I began to understand that matters of race and racism were paramount to understanding how people relate to others in their families, communities, even worldwide. I also believe that until this idea is truly explored, we educators will continue to perpetuate racism and misunderstand issues of race.

❖   ❖   ❖

What are your reactions to Dorothy's and Bonnie's racial histories?

_____

_____

_____

_____

_____

Try the following exercises, first alone, then with others:

Write your racial past. Write a history that includes the interactions that you have had with people of a different color from yourself. You may choose to draw a timeline rather than write your racial history.

_____

_____

_____

_____

_____

_____

_____

_____

_____

**What compelling differences do you find in your racial autobiography
and the autobiography of others?**

_____

_____

_____

_____

**Considering the challenges others face, what things might you do
differently in the future?**

_____

_____

_____

_____

THE ONGOING JOURNEY

Having close friends who possess different racial pasts helps me understand
better my own myopic view. Each day I learn something new, often I am embarrassed by my ignorance, seldom do I feel smug. Usually I feel humbled and wish
knowledge didn't hurt so much.

For example, the name we use to call others is very important, and I always
attempt to respect the name any one person and any group wishes to be called.

I had been using the term *Hispanic* for people of color who are from Mexico, South America, and the Caribbean islands. Then a colleague told me that the term was disrespectful and applied only to people of Spanish origin. She said to use the term *Latino/a*.

I went through my materials and changed all the Hispanic references to Latino/a. I felt good.

Weeks later, an educator in Houston, Texas, asked me to present to her district. She told me their student body was 50% Hispanic. When I told her I had some Latino/a bibliographies, she informed me that the term was *Hispanic*, not *Latino/a*. I told her I had just changed all my materials from *Hispanic* to *Latino/a*. She replied that in her area, people use the term *Hispanic*.

I have yet to solve this dilemma, but a strategy I now use is to ask people what they want to be called. I know that some people of color of African descent choose to be called African American and some choose to be called Black. Some people prefer to be called Latino/a, while others prefer Hispanic. When I present to a new faculty, I now do some research and try to find out the term used in the area; if I am unsuccessful, I use both terms, and if I am to continue working with them, I ask them which term they prefer. This is easy to do with a student also. It is no different from asking a child whether he wants to be called James or Jim. It is critical to use the appellations for others that best match their authentic selves.

"Naming" is a topic that can provoke a meaningful conversation. Because conquered people have seldom been allowed the luxury of naming themselves, they should be allowed the respect we give any group and call them by the name they now choose to be called. Recently, in Vancouver, several educators explained their chosen appellation—First Nation People. What an honorable term for the original inhabitants of a country.

Reflect on your "fatigue level" upon completing this chapter. Do you find it tiring to think about your racial past and others' racial identities?

_____

_____

_____

_____

If you are White, can you better understand how tiring it might be to have to deal with your racial identity 100% of the time? Even though we each are impacted by our race 100% of the time (Singleton & Linton, 2006), I can choose to walk away from it and not have to think about it as I move about in our White-dominated society until I encounter a person of color.

In the next chapter, you will read about a day in the life of these two educators. Once again, these examples are not representative of entire groups but rather illustrate the diverse experiences each of us lives. The more we know and understand about the diversity of our students' daily experiences, the more equipped we are to understand their perspectives and act accordingly.

❖ ❖ ❖

SUGGESTED READING

Delgado, Richard, and Jean Stefancic. 1997. *Critical White Studies: Looking Behind the Mirror.*

Landsman, Julie. 2001. *A White Teacher Talks About Race.*

McIntyre, Alice. 1997. *Making Meaning of Whiteness: Exploring Racial Identity With White Teachers.*

6

A Day in the Life . . .

This chapter discusses White privilege. If you are reading this as a White person, do you possess privilege denied to educators and students who are not classified as White? This chapter examines this issue by describing Bonnie's and Dorothy's days and compares their experiences as a White woman and as a woman who is not classified as White. Prompts follow to give you an opportunity to reflect on your experiences.

If I, as a White educator, do not understand what Whiteness brings to my diverse classroom, I lack important information. What does it mean to be White in America? Researchers have written about White privilege, yet when I bring it up during workshops, most White people are surprised with this concept. No surprise, for if I am White, I don't have to think about it unless I choose to put myself into a minority position or am forced into one. Yet people of color do not have that option. Glenn Singleton states that each morning he looks out the window as a Black man, while I, as a White person, look out the window as just a person (Singleton, 2003).

WHITE PRIVILEGE

In "White Privilege and Male Privilege: A Personal Account of Coming to See Correspondences Through Work in Women's Studies," Peggy McIntosh (1998), women studies professor at Wellesley College, defines White privilege as an "invisible package of unearned assets which I can count on cashing in each day, but about which I was 'meant' to remain oblivious" (p. 291). McIntosh cites 54 privileges that Whites use daily as "an invisible weightless knapsack of special provisions" (cited in Delgado & Stefancic, 1997, p. 292). In this White-dominated society, I wear my Whiteness as an invisible protection each moment of my life.

Think about your day. Do you daily receive privilege due to your skin color? Or do you daily confront the challenges outlined by Dorothy, a woman of color?

Dorothy, as an African American, does not represent *all* persons of cultures who are not classified as White; however, her experiences hold a mirror up to White privilege. Let's examine the invisible privilege package that I, a White woman, wear in a typical day in my life.

A DAY IN BONNIE'S LIFE

I awake. I read the paper and watch the television news where I see White men portrayed as the authority, full of confidence, with a vocal style that matches mine. My speaking patterns are reinforced—they refer to their mothers as "Mother" or "Mom," not "Mama" or "Mum." Their vocabulary, even their accent, matches my middle-class White, midwestern self. I drive to work.

Mostly I pass Whites driving cars as I drive from a suburb up a superhighway that stretches through the middle of St. Louis to the University of Missouri. I see passengers of my own color in the majority of the cars.

At the building where I work, there are approximately 25 people. Four are African American women, three of whom are support personnel. None is Asian. None is a Black male. None is Hispanic. I am reinforced throughout my day that my culture is in charge, correct, and successful.

After work I drive to a fitness center where I work out. Usually one or two African Americans work out too, but the interesting thing is that all of the cleaning people and the service people in the coffee shop are Black. The only Black person in the spa section is the receptionist, a light-skinned woman with long, flowing hair. My subconscious mind sees that Blacks clean the toilets at the fitness center, Whites and one Asian do the massages and the nails.

I drive home to a neighborhood block that is 80% White. There are a few neighbors who are people of color. One biracial woman is married to a White male; others are Asian and Hispanic. One is a Black male.

I watch the 5:00 p.m. news. The anchors are White; the important news usually revolves around Whites, usually males. Stories of violence mostly depict Blacks.

My friends are mostly middle-class White women like me. My significant other is a White male. I don't have to worry about being followed by security at the local shopping mall; I don't have to worry about being stopped by the police because of my skin color. I don't have to worry about being invisible in my community. I am acknowledged when I walk up to a counter, whether it is a fast-food place, the cleaners, the video counter, or the local school.

I am White. I have unearned power because of my skin color.

In what ways is your day similar to mine?

_____

_____

_____

Think about your students of color. In what ways might their days differ from yours?

_____

_____

_____

Dorothy's day differs from mine in many ways. As you read her account, think about the differences.

A DAY IN DOROTHY'S LIFE

In this "White" or "dominant culture" society, I feel like I wear my Blackness as an offense to some people. I do not have just one typical day, because for me the days are a continuum of responses to race and racism. I do not have any protection against what I may encounter—I simply have the wisdom of a warrior.

When I wake up, I view the news and hear what seems to be endless accounts of Black on Black crime. I see sad mug shots of Black folk, mostly males, and always there is commentary from a family member or bystander. I often cringe, hoping not to hear the name of a former student or one of their family members. I have recognized several over the past 20 years.

Despite how my day starts, I manage to make it to the neighborhood coffee shop, pick up coffee, and drive to work pretty happy about what I might encounter. Although I live in an integrated community, I rarely see any people of color at the coffee shop, not any Asians, Latinos/as, or African Americans— just White barristers and customers. Currently, my workplace has 14 people of color: 12 African Americans and 2 Chinese. The remaining 100 employees are White. I am one of two African American administrators in the school district. Previously, I worked as the first and only African American administrator for over 10 years, and I was the single African American employee in my building for the duration of my tenure with the district. I presume now I work with an ethnically diverse staff.

I am challenged on personal and professional levels by issues of race and racism. The challenges do not happen every day, but I have been challenged so many times that there is no doubt to me and to whoever is privy to the "onslaught" that it is indeed about my being African American and it is undeniably about race or racism. My decisions may be questioned or second-guessed by the staff members whom I supervise. My ideas sometimes seem to be dismissed or not perceived as legitimate explanations surrounding matters of African American student achievement by my fellow administrators. White parents comfortably insult Black students or me by using racial slurs and blatant stereotypes when discussing matters of conflict between their child and a student of color or teacher of color. In turn, Black parents comfortably challenge my racial identity or Blackness when they disagree with a decision I have made about their son or daughter who is involved in a conflict with a White student or White teacher.

Another insult that I occasionally encounter is that I'm called "nigger" by a White parent who is angry. I have encountered racial slurs numerous times: "nigger," "Black bitch," "jiggaboo," "you're just one of them." Equally disturbing, I'm also called some of these racial slurs by African American parents. I have been told by an angry White parent after I suspended her son for fighting that the KKK is watching how I treat White kids. I have been told by a White teacher that I would not be allowed to observe her or I would be sued. I have been told by a White teacher that I better not come into her room or she would report me to the board of education. I have been jokingly told by a White teacher that when the desegregation program started, she had to take down a sign in her room that said "No administrators and no niggers allowed." While sitting with a group of Black employees at my current job, I have been teased by a White teacher that we are planning a conspiracy together, yet White teachers sit together all the time without fear of being alluded to as conspirators. As an administrator, I try to be professional, friendly, and respectful to everyone. I walk a balance beam because of my supervisory role, and I have to hold back on a personal level because by being a Black supervisor, you are always in fear of being removed from your job. This is a common belief among African American administrators or supervisors in most fields. You have an uneasy feeling that others, especially White people, believe you were hired because you are Black, and you fear you will be fired (laid off, phased out, downsized) because you are Black. I also find in talking with other African Americans that we get the "Black" problems whether they are one of our students or not. And no one wants to admit to that particular phenomenon.

The best encounters during my days are with the students. At times it is hard for students to put their feelings of discrimination into words—they just know they were treated unfairly. A teacher may scold them for disruptive behaviors that White students are not reprimanded for by the same White teacher. They may fail classes even though they have completed all the assignments and received passing grades on all those assignments but fail or achieve low test scores. They cannot find any other explanation for the F, nor can their parents. African American students and other students of color complain of racism when a White teacher or a White student makes a racially insensitive remark or joke and no one intervenes. I understand that I'm working with middle school students, and their sense of fairness is skewed at times, but I also understand when issues of race or racism are present. In turn, I understand that many White teachers are uncomfortable, untrained, and unable to talk about matters of race and racism.

My Day as an African American

My day as an African American runs on a continuum to the degree that I encounter race and racism—not because it's one day, one morning, or one afternoon; it is ongoing day after day and year after year. Even in my personal life, I have endured humiliating racial incidents such as not getting served in a restaurant or standing at a counter for several minutes when a White male or female butts in front of me and gets immediate service. I can be smartly dressed or casually dressed and I'm somehow still invisible. It makes me wonder who really is ignoring me, the person who butts in front of me or the service person who is supposed to be waiting on me. Perhaps the worst is when, for some unknown reason, a White person will drive by and holler out a racial slur at me—I can only pray that a physical attack does not take place next. Sometimes I keep track of this by marking the date it occurred, but eventually I get discouraged, and I think to myself, Don't keep a record of racism, because it only increases the tension and stress that goes with being a Black person.

As my day ends and as I mature in my career, I appreciate the drive home and entering the safe place where I can momentarily think of things that are not about race and racism.

UNDERSTANDING PRIVILEGE

What differences did you find in Dorothy's day and in Bonnie's day?

_____

_____

_____

_____

_____

What responsibility do you have to learn about the experiences that other cultures confront daily?

_____

_____

_____

_____

_____

What responsibility do you have to examine your own privilege in every decision that is made in your educational setting?

_____

_____

_____

_____

What responsibility do you have to examine the privilege of White children in every decision that is made in your educational setting?

_____

_____

_____

_____

Do you understand how and when _privilege_ is used as a verb in your school setting? For example, when a tuxedo business asked six senior boys to model tuxedos for the students during their lunch periods and not one young man of color was asked to participate, I went to the administration and complained. The administrators understood, and that is all it took to remedy the situation. Sometimes we just need a set of eyes to call to the attention of well-meaning folks what they do not see. Unfortunately, if a person of color had complained, they might have been judged as being overly sensitive.

What are some ways that you can make yourself accountable for privileging all children?

_____

_____

_____

_____

If you are a person of the dominant culture, can you call attention to oversights, conscious or subconscious, in order to be self-accountable?

_____

_____

_____

_____

_____

What have you learned as a result of reading this chapter?

_____

_____

_____

_____

This chapter has examined two educators' days in an attempt to add another dimension, that of White privilege, to our understanding of what some educators bring to the classroom. Throughout the first six chapters in this book, we have examined culture, research on diverse learners, the issue of the achievement gap, racial histories, and the impact of race in our daily lives. The remainder of the chapters in the book examine classroom instruction and focus on the strategies we can implement to improve student achievement.

❖   ❖   ❖

SUGGESTED READING

Delgado, Richard, and Jean Stafancic. 1997. _Critical White Studies: Looking Behind the Mirror._

Landsman, Julie. 2001. _A White Teacher Talks About Race._

McIntyre, Alice. 1997. _Making Meaning of Whiteness: Exploring Racial Identity With White Teachers._

Singleton, Glenn E., and Curtis Linton. 2006. _Courageous Conversations About Race._

PART III

Creating a Learning Environment That Supports Diverse Learners

7

Building Community Through Research-Based Learning Expectations

BEHAVIOR EXPECTATIONS

The next several chapters describe the learning environment necessary to build a classroom of excellence. Chapter 7 begins with building a classroom community and what that entails. Chapter 8 widens the classroom community to the school culture or community and discusses ways to welcome diverse learners. Chapter 9 offers suggestions for using books to build a literate school and community culture. Chapter 10 ends this section with suggestions and strategies for building relationships with diverse learners. This section of the book examines closely the affective aspect of learning and what we teachers can do to create a learning environment conducive to rigorous content instruction.

To begin, students must understand what is expected of them. Many students just seem to "know" what to do and expect in our classrooms; however, others, often our diverse learners, may not be privy to the hidden rules or codes of our classrooms. We who possess the knowledge of our hidden rules are the gatekeepers to success or failure for those who do not possess the knowledge (Delpit, 1997). Because of this, we must be sensitive to the cultural lenses of our diverse learners and create an equitable field of opportunity for all.

In order to have an equitable playing field of opportunity, we have to clearly state our behavior expectations for the task at hand. In discussions, many adults and students hesitate to give input when the discussion focuses on such scary subjects as race, class, gender, or culture. Many remain silent rather than risk offending another human being.

During a workshop, the presenter can present norms and boundaries, model them, and set the tone for the presentation. This is good teaching. It also gives the presenter the authority to intervene if a participant interrupts another speaker or speaks out of turn. In other words, the presenter states explicitly the expected "hidden rules" or "code" of an educational setting. The teacher must do the same in the classroom.

You might find the following expectations when you attend a workshop:

Today, we will examine issues that challenge us to think deeply and respond honestly. We need to agree to follow behavior expectations.

- Take care of yourself. If you need to leave the room, do so. (Obviously, this one is for participants in a presentation or workshop, not your classroom.)

- Safeguard your reflective time by remaining quiet, then share during sharing time.

- Listen deeply. Do not interrupt anyone who is speaking. Wait until the person has completed his or her statements.

- Do not hog airtime. Share airtime equally with your colleagues. Each person has unique and valuable comments to contribute.

- Leave your outside concerns outside the room. Focus deeply on the stated topic.

- Save a few minutes during your break just for yourself—take a short walk, stand alone and think, be alone. Reflection encourages new learning.

- Do not stereotype people or their actions when you discuss the issues. Instead, use qualifying words. For example, use these words when appropriate: *few, some, sometimes, I've observed.* Do not use *most, all of the time,* or make stereo-typical, generalized statements. When we describe the actions of others who differ from us, we will refrain from language which stereotypes others.

- Remember that each of us has lived a unique life. No one can ever know exactly what your experiences have felt like for you, and you can never know exactly what another person has experienced. Therefore, use only *I* messages and *do not* tell any other person what his or her experience has been. Don't even tell another person that you know what he or she is feeling. This can be especially offensive to a person of color if you are a White person who says, "I know exactly what you're feeling." I, as a member of the dominant group in the United States, can never really know what it is like to be a member of a nondominant group.

- Give this experience your best. Our society seldom provides a forum for us to speak frankly about the effects of race, class, culture, and gender upon one's life experiences. Do not be surprised if you feel uncomfortable during some of the discussion. Glenn Singleton and Curtis Linton (2006) remind us that when discussing issues of race, we will feel uncomfortable and experience no closure. For many of us who want to "do" or "fix" things, this is unsettling; however, such discussions are about learning more of what we don't know we don't know, rather than fixing the situation.

- Respect each other's privacy. Please do not share the personal comments made during your discussions outside the workshop or classroom.

By following these expectations, you will leave this experience with a new respect for the other participants and, hopefully, closer relationships with them.

Generate some behavior expectations for your interactions with your colleagues and/or your students.

_____

_____

_____

ESTABLISHING BEHAVIOR EXPECTATIONS

Establishing behavior expectations for professional development discussions is valuable, but you may be more interested in establishing codes of behavior for your classroom. Have you tried using rules, only to find that you can never make enough rules to cover every situation? Often, a long list of rules simply confuses both students and the teacher. Jacqueline Woodbury (1997) suggests using just five statements for effective classroom discipline. She divides them into rights and responsibilities. Her rights include the right to be safe and to learn. Her responsibilities include the responsibility to be polite, to be honest, and to use time wisely. Using these five guidelines, students can generate "above-the-line" and "below-the-line" behaviors that fall within each one. For example, a student who talks to another student while the teacher is attempting to teach violates the right to learn and the responsibility to be polite. Correcting the student is an opportunity to teach the class the expected above-the-line behavior rather than a chance to be punitive. You might ask the student, "John, that is a below-the-line behavior. What is the above-the-line-behavior?" John says, "Sit quietly and listen to the teacher." John tells his brain, in an affirmative manner, what he should be doing in order to learn, one of his rights. These five statements cover all behaviors, unlike a list of rules that can never cover all.

These statements are also general enough that they allow you to apply them based on the individual needs of each student. One study found that the most effective teachers use different classroom management strategies with different types of students, while ineffective teachers do not. Effective teachers do not treat all students the same, especially surrounding issues of behavior. Some students respond better to encouragement, others need a gentle reprimand, and others need more intervention (Marzano, 2003).

Finally, some behavior expectation programs, rather than focusing on student behavior change, examine teacher behaviors and suggest ways for teachers to improve their skills in classroom management. One such program is Teacher Expectations, Student Achievement (TESA), which examines 15 teacher behaviors and has a peer-observation component. Another is *Conscious Discipline: 7 Basic Skills for Brain Smart Classroom Management* by Becky Bailey (2001). This program is built on three major premises: "Controlling and changing ourselves is possible and has profound impact on others; connectedness governs behavior; and conflict is an opportunity to teach" (p. 13). If we conduct our classrooms with a positive mental intention and use discipline infractions as opportunities to teach social skills to our students, we lay the foundation for effective instruction.

A COMMUNITY OF LEARNERS

Think about a time when you walked into a room and felt uncomfortable. Was it because you were an outsider? You may have found yourself not thinking as clearly as you usually do or worrying about how others perceive you rather than focusing on the reason why you were there. Are you behaving in a "culturally appropriate" manner? In *A Biological Brain in a Cultural Classroom*, Robert Sylwester (2000) states that "culturally appropriate is something we constantly negotiate in our own life and in our interactions with others" (p. 135). So how do culturally diverse learners negotiate the culture of your classroom?

Diverse learners successfully negotiate the culture of your classroom when they feel part of a community. Think about how much easier it is to function when you feel part of the community, whether that is your family, your classroom, your church, or your school. Creating community is essential to the learning environment (Sousa, 2001). Sousa states that "learning occurs more easily in environments free from threat or intimidation" (p. 61); therefore, we must establish a safe community where students do not fear ridicule, embarrassment, failure, or physical threat.

WHAT IS COMMUNITY?

Community is where you feel accepted and loved. It is where you feel your voice counts. The opposite is when you feel invisible and isolated. When students feel unloved and invisible in our classroom community, we can expect social instability and inappropriate behavior. As adolescents, they may create their own cultures, such as classroom cliques and gangs, to provide them with the opportunities to succeed within a community, no matter how adverse it is to the mainstream community of the classroom (Sylwester, 2000). Therefore, if we need people to care about others in order to create community, how do we build community?

Students need to know they are welcome in our classrooms and that they are responsible for their own learning and their behaviors. We need to create a climate where each child feels welcomed. In addition, we must believe in the potential of each student and work to unleash that potential

(Gregory & Chapman, 2002). When students are not functioning well in our classroom, we might ask if the climate is conducive to learning. Are basic needs being met? In addition to the physiological needs we all have, there are psychological needs, and an important psychological need is the need to belong (Bailey, 2000; Gregory & Chapman, 2002).

Recently, during a professional development workshop, one fifth-grade teacher asked another, "What did you do last year? You didn't send one student to the office for misbehavior." The other answered, "I spent most of the first two weeks building community in my classroom."

By investing time in building classroom community, the whole class benefited in time *not* lost on discipline-related problems, and it paid off in positive student behavior for all.

You can choose several strategies, but the community you build must reflect your needs and those of your particular students. You, the teacher, must find out the "who" of each class, the personality of each group, before you create your community. Some groups define themselves quickly; others evolve more slowly. You the teacher, too, are part of the equation and make up the who that teaches (Palmer, 1998). Establishing rights and responsibilities or a common statement of values encourages your classroom community to grow and flourish.

What will you do now to create a classroom community?

_____

_____

_____

DEVELOPING BEHAVIOR EXPECTATIONS

You will want behavior expectations for each classroom activity. Below is an exercise you might use to develop these for group work. Begin this activity with a role-modeling exercise. Role-playing provides an especially good opportunity for memory retention, a file folder of sorts, because it is connected to real-life experiences (Sylwester, 2000). Have two or three students join you in front of the class and go through the following questions together. Tell the students to give serious answers, since they are the models for this activity.

How shall we treat each other whenever we interact together?

_____

_____

_____

Step One:

Think about your expectations when you interact with others. Write down three expectations you have of others when working in a group.

_____

_____

_____

Step Two:

Share at your table. As a group, decide upon the two expectations that are most important to observe when working together.

_____

_____

_____

Step Three:

As a group, list the expectations expressed by each table. Optional: Prioritize.

_____

_____

_____

Step Four:

Discuss the implications of this exercise. What did you learn about yourself during this exercise? How can it apply this year to your feeling safe in this classroom? How does it support your learning?

_____

_____

_____

Allow the students to practice in their groups. Come to a consensus with the entire class. Post your expectations on the wall. If you are teaching middle or high school, you will have a different list for each class. Have the students who enjoy art decorate them. Use these to begin building an environment that reflects your classroom community.

Follow the classroom exercise with a discussion of rights and responsibilities.

Sylwester (2000) suggests beginning each day by asking your students how they feel. Using a scale of points or "good-bad," you can determine your students' moods and respond appropriately. Have you ever noticed how your students, after you have shared that you are not feeling well or have a family crisis, will behave exceptionally well? They are responding to your sharing your mood, just as each member of the classroom community can respond to the overall mood of the group.

Explicitly teaching our students that the only thing we can really control is our own behavior leads to building a community that respects the learning of all.

The following are suggestions for building community in your classroom.

Twenty-one Tools for Building Community
Level: Elementary/Middle/High
Subject: Cross-curricular

1. Recognize or celebrate students' birthdays.
2. Fill your classroom with plants. Include those that flower in winter so that students can anticipate the event.
3. Give each student a particular responsibility in the classroom. Kays (quoted in Sylwester, 2000) found that one factor in Grades 4 and 5 at-risk students' feelings of alienation from school occurred because teachers did not assign them routine classroom tasks at the same rate as the other students in the classroom. Rotate these responsibilities.
4. Work on a community service event as a class—this is an outstanding way to bond a class.
5. Do a gratitude journal together as a class.
6. Write and illustrate a class book.
7. Take pictures of the class and post them on the walls. Include pictures of your family; students love to know about you as a person.
8. Do a student-of-the-week bulletin board.
9. Invite the students who enjoy art to hang samples of their work around the classroom.
10. Post a reading list for each student in the class.
11. Bring healthy food as a treat—apples, dried fruit, nuts. Investigate whether you can have water in your classroom.
12. Smile! Use humor!
13. Use your alphabetical attendance list and ask one child per day about an interest he or she has that has nothing to do with school. You should get to each child one time per month this way.

---

14. Make one positive parent phone call per day. Leave a message on the answering machine if you cannot reach the parents.

15. Take your class on a field trip.

16. Connect with a retirement home and have students interview residents and then write their stories.

17. Keep a pet in the classroom, if appropriate.

18. Ask students to share their stories.

19. Have students give talks about their favorite books.

20. Have each child bring in an object and tell the class why it is meaningful to him or her.

21. Have each child do a biographical poster, collage, or mobile and then share with the class during the first week. Afterward, post each one in the room and tell your students that the space their project occupies belongs to them. Consider allowing them to own that space all year, continuing to change the materials, if they choose.

School Experiences to Welcome Caregivers and Families of Diverse Learners

- Produce a Writers' Showcase where students read their writings to the parents. Invite parents to attend during the hour that their children have English. You can use a library, a theater, or your classroom. You can have snacks and make it as formal as you like. Encourage students to do most of the planning and preparation: one can type the program with the reading order of the students, one can draw a picture for the cover of the program, several can bring treats, some can make phone calls to check on attendance, and so on. This is a wonderful way to include all students and many caregivers. For working caregivers, you may want to hold the program at night.

- Offer English as a Second Language classes for adults.

- Put on a Family Treasures Night with a potluck dinner and ask families to bring a dish that is special to their family.

- Hold an International Night as the culmination of students' research projects.

- Have an Oral History Night and invite grandparents and parents to speak about their participation in past historical events.

- Hold a schoolwide book club for families (see Chapter 9).

- Invite parents to create a parents' room in the school. Fill the room with books on parenting and school success. Add a microwave, a coffeemaker, some food and drink. Then invite them to inhabit it. One school received a grant to create this kind of space, and parents have responded enthusiastically.

- Consider adult education experiences such as computer training.

- Hold study/homework sessions after school for families.

- Hold a school rummage sale.

- Create a family/school garden. A lovely garden welcomes all who step through the school's doors.

Which strategies might you adopt to create a community of learners?

_____

_____

_____

This chapter outlined how we can work together to create a classroom of academic excellence, honoring and supporting all students. In Chapter 8 are some scenarios that depict three different school districts for you to read about and assess the effectiveness of their school cultures.

SUGGESTED READING

Bailey, Becky. 2000. _Conscious Discipline: 7 Basic Skills for Brain Smart Classroom Management._

Marzano, Robert. 2003. _Classroom Management That Works._

Sylwester, Robert. 2000. _A Biological Brain in a Cultural Classroom: Applying Biological Research to Classroom Management._

Tomlinson, Carol Ann. 2003. _Fulfilling the Promise of the Differentiated Classroom._

8

Creating a School Culture That Welcomes Diverse Learners

How do we build a school culture to welcome diverse learners? Nearly every school has one or more isolated classrooms that welcome diverse learners, yet one classroom of excellence does not create an excellent school. To create a school of excellence, a positive, academic culture must flourish. This chapter examines the concept of school culture and its impact upon diverse learners.

School culture is extremely important. It shapes the norms of the environment. It says what's cool and what's in. If that culture is one of academic rigor, then that's cool; that's the goal. By achieving, students are buying into the culture, into their environment of acceptance. By failing, they are failures of that culture. A student's perceived acceptance into the school culture directly affects his or her motivation to achieve.

Both teachers and students can be caught in a perceived reality that keeps each individual from attaining his or her potential (Lindsey, Roberts, & CampbellJones, 2005). Garcia (quoted in Artiles & Ortiz, 2002) suggests that in order for diverse learners to feel included in the academic school culture, teachers must see their cultural differences as assets to their achievement, rather than as deficits to be modified by the dominant culture.

How do you rate the academic culture of your school?

_____

_____

_____

Read the following scenarios and think about the culture in each of these school districts. How do you think the culture might impact student achievement?

_____

_____

_____

SCHOOL DISTRICT A

In School District A, students are taught and supported and expected to attend the local community college, the state universities, or no college at all. Fewer than 50% attend college. There seldom is a National Merit Scholar finalist. District scores usually fall just above the median score on state tests. The students are respectful, follow middle-class rules, and mostly do what they are told. Sports are important in the schools, and morning announcements in the secondary schools often center on school sports events. The schools are kept clean and have adequate technology and support help. There is a general mistrust of the administration by the teachers, and a "we versus them" attitude exists, yet teachers usually have the resources they need and are generally satisfied and do an adequate job. Teachers seldom leave; in fact, several teachers attended as children the very schools in which they now teach. The community surrounding the school is comprised of several generations of families with similar religious and ethnic backgrounds. Diversity is usually not welcomed in the schools, and newcomers are expected to assimilate quickly in order to be successful in their new surrounding.

SCHOOL DISTRICT B

In School District B, students often enter from the impoverished neighborhoods in a large urban area. The student population primarily consists of students of color; however, the majority of the teaching staff is White. Students are expected to drop out, attend local technical schools or a community college, or pursue no advanced schooling. District scores on state tests fall far below the median scores except at the district magnet schools. Schools are kept clean, yet facilities vary from severely lacking to adequate. In some schools, one finds such challenges as adult bathrooms without locks, ceilings that leak rain on students' heads, lack of breakfast for every hungry child, young students forced to stand outside in the bitter cold waiting in lines to go through metal detectors, broken desks, inadequate or lack of necessary supplies, and a lack of access to technology. Teacher mistrust is high because teachers are often treated as children as in a "parent-child" relationship, being told what to do and how to do it as though they lack efficacy. The teachers union is strong, and the administration and the union are often at odds. Teachers are often moved from school to school, and often they teach next door to uncertified staff or substitute teachers. It is not unusual to find teachers teaching core subjects without a college major in the area. Students in the schools are orderly or disruptive, depending upon the administration at each building. Yet even in the most orderly of buildings, students seldom reach high levels of academic rigor. Teacher expectations and student expectations often wane with each passing year, and seniors find themselves unprepared for college and unable to compete with students from districts that lie within five miles of their schools.

SCHOOL DISTRICT C

In School District C, the schools are reputed to be among the best in the state. District scores rank at top levels, and 99% of the high school graduates attend college. From kindergarten on, there is an expectation that students will attend an Ivy League school or a private liberal arts college in another state, preferably on the East Coast. Students are challenged from the day they enter school, and the evidence of academic success permeates the entire district. Academic rituals abound in this district. Juniors are involved in a lengthy awards ceremony where alumni/ae of Ivy League schools give book awards to the most promising students. Students are usually involved in several extracurricular academic activities outside of school. Koman math, music study with symphony performers, Sylvan Learning Centers, weekly tutors, and additional foreign language classes are common evening activities for the district's children. Sports are important, but all-inclusive, so a student can be a member of any sports team, regardless of ability. Schools are clean but not necessarily more modern or better equipped than in School District A. The priority is obviously not on the facilities but on the learning that takes place inside. Teachers usually have master's degrees in their content area and often consider it a failing of theirs if a child does not succeed. There is a high degree of efficacy on the part of the teachers and most students. There is a sense that "we're all in this together." Morning announcements focus on academic successes, and a day seldom goes by when one does not hear of a student or entire student group winning a prestigious award. Administrators generally treat teachers as equals and as adults capable of making important classroom decisions. Teachers work in collaboration and continuously refine their practice through professional development and self-study. From the moment a student enters the halls of this district's schools, he or she knows that college means another step toward personal and economic success. Students learn how to play the stock market, do out-of-state college visits during their junior year, and are carefully directed by a college counselor. Diversity is valued. Students mix in social groups, and many have traveled to other countries and even lived there. African American students who attend this school system through a voluntary, court-regulated desegregation program enter this world of academic expectations. The result? The achievement gap is more narrow in this district than in most other districts involved in the desegregation program. Why? For a variety of reasons, although one is climate, the school culture of academic excellence. Buying into this culture brings acceptance, not alienation.

Reflect on the three scenarios and list why you think School District C has higher achievement:

_____

_____

_____

What can you do to establish a school culture of academic excellence?

_____

_____

_____

The following are some suggestions.

**Level: Elementary/Middle/High School
Subject: Cross-curricular**

- Use professional mentors from the community (Elementary/Middle/High).
- For role models, post pictures of people of color in various professions (Elementary/Middle/High).
- Ask retired teachers to volunteer in schools to provide time for teacher collaboration (Elementary/Middle/High).
- Post visuals of universities in the halls and public places (Elementary/Middle/High).

- Organize orientations for students and parents that revolve around college placement and financial aid (Middle/High).
- Encourage staff to share their stories of how, when, and why they attended college (Elementary/Middle/High).
- Have staff mentor students (Elementary/Middle/High).
- Have college recruiters visit and meet with students during their sophomore year (High).
- Administer the PSAT to students in English classes during their sophomore year and go over the test with all students, teaching them test-taking strategies (High).
- Require English teachers to teach the SAT/ACT vocabulary lists as a regular part of their classes (High).
- Have English teachers assign the college essay as one of their regular assignments during Grades 10, 11, and 12. Have contests celebrating the best. Consider having the students read their essays over the public address system on occasion (High).
- Have English teachers mentor students through the college application process. Use the English research paper to investigate college choices (High).

Describe the current culture of your school.

_____

_____

_____

_____

How does that culture influence you?

_____

_____

_____

_____

What positive steps can you take to influence the culture of your school?

_____

_____

_____

_____

Design a plan to develop a more rigorous academic culture in your school.

_____

_____

_____

_____

In this chapter, you examined whole-school culture. The challenge to create an academic whole-school culture is formidable. One school district accomplished this task by using books to build school and community relationships, then built upon these relationships to increase the academic achievement of its students. The next chapter describes how your district might use books to build a whole-school or whole-district academic culture.

❖ ❖ ❖

SUGGESTED READING

Gregory, Gayle, and Carolyn Chapman. 2002. _Differentiated Instructional Strategies: One Size Doesn't Fit All._
Sylwester, Robert. 2000. _A Biological Brain in a Cultural Classroom._

9

Using Books to Support School and Community Partnerships

Educators sometimes speak about the lack of involvement of students' families with the schools. Parents or caregivers may not trust us until they know us and believe that we know them. So how do we get to know our students' families? Why not hold an all-district or whole-school book study for your families? Connecting to families may then be as easy as sharing a book and discussing its story. When discussing a book, such as those listed in this chapter, educators and families can share their personal stories and everyone involved gets to know each other just a little more than when they walked through the door. A school book study can bridge the chasm between school and the home, between educator and the parent.

Books are truly bridges to understanding others, yet in the past, teachers have often communicated to their students that they need some superior intelligence to tell them what the book means that they are reading (Wilhelm, 1995). However, if we do not help students find meaning in their reading experience and make connections to their own lives, we are in danger of being dishonest and of creating a cynical and disaffected community in our classrooms (Chambers, 1985). And cynical and disaffected students often act out and disengage. First we have to connect to the lives of our students and their families.

If you want a book to connect to students and their families, try *Seedfolks* (Fleischman, 1997). This award-winning book can build community in an upper-level elementary school classroom, a middle school classroom, a high school classroom, a college classroom, a school, and/or an entire community.

This is one of several books that a local middle/high school has used in their community book club. Others the district used in the past two years have been *Stargirl* (Spinelli, 2000), *Stuck in Neutral* (Trueman, 2000), *Among the Hidden* (Haddix, 1998), and *Whirligig* (Fleischman, 1998). Each of these books fits into the genre of young adult (YA) literature, and the books appeal to both adolescents and adults. Two to four times a year, the book club offers a light supper and invites the community to spend the evening discussing the chosen book. If you need sources for funding, contact your PTO, ask local businesses, write grants, or ask for money from the district's budget.

After choosing a book, perhaps from the list above, you may consider using it in one of the following ways:

- Use this book for an all-school read-a-thon.
- Read it over the intercom.
- Have students choose a character/chapter to share with the class.
- Use it as a professional development activity to begin your year.

A book study is a powerful tool to use with your staff. When you have a professional development day, you might consider using a book to focus your discussion. *Seedfolks* is an outstanding book to use. The following prompts were developed to use with the book. No matter what book you choose, you can create your own prompts for discussion.

SEEDFOLKS PROMPTS

Share why you became an educator or a professional who has chosen to work in a school setting.

_____

_____

_____

Reflect upon your garden history. Use the following prompts to craft your story:

- When you were a child, did your family have a garden?
- If yes, who tended the garden?

- Did you take part in the tending of the garden?
- What kind of garden was it?

_____

_____

_____

_____

_____

_____

Was it a significant part of your childhood?

_____

_____

During your adult years, have you had a garden?

_____

_____

If so, what kind of garden have you had and how significant is it to you?

_____

_____

_____

A GARDEN HISTORY ACTIVITY FOR STAFF AND COMMUNITY MEMBERS

Give staff members a sheet of chart paper and ask them to write about and/or illustrate their garden history, which is their personal story about what part a garden played in their childhood, adolescence, and adulthood. For example, their families might have planted gardens, and they might have worked in them as children. Or perhaps they created gardens as adults.

Use 15 minutes or so to write/illustrate the garden history. Then, in groups of three or four staff members, share the garden histories. Sharing personal stories builds the sense of community among the staff and sets a positive tone for the school year.

You may want your staff to consider the following questions/reflections:

How is a gardener like a teacher?

_____

_____

_____

How is a gardener like a student?

_____

_____

_____

What skills does a teacher need that a gifted gardener possesses?

_____

_____

_____

What skills does a student need that a gifted gardener possesses?

_____

_____

_____

Ask parents/community members questions such as these or generate your own:

How is your role in your family like a gardener?

_____

_____

_____

Does your family "grow" in cycles similar to the seasons of a garden? (This one pushes participants to think metaphorically and can result in a deeper exchange between members of the book group.)

_____

_____

_____

READING FICTION AND PARTICIPATING IN INFORMAL DISCUSSIONS

At the elementary level, you may choose a different format when you use books to connect to students and families. One elementary school visits each student's place of residence during the summer and, after interacting with the family, leaves a gift bag that includes books and school supplies. Imagine how far ahead this school is regarding relationships with students and their families. Another elementary school holds literacy nights where families share poetry, children's books, and stories. The principal sends a bus to pick up families (not a school bus, but a double-decker bus that a local business owns and donates for the evenings).

By involving your students and their families with books that speak to them, you build bridges across cultures that demonstrate caring and compassion. The ways you involve the families of your students is limited only by your imagination.

This chapter described whole-school book studies that reach students and their families. But what about each individual student? How do you build a relationship of mutual respect with each student in your classroom? The next chapter outlines relationship strategies to use with your students as you build your classroom of excellence.

10

Cultivating Relationships With Diverse Learners

Have you noticed that there are some teachers who students just love? What is their secret? What do these teachers do to build relationships with individual students? This chapter offers you an opportunity to ponder your relationship-building skills and suggests numerous strategies based on the research to build relationships with your students.

When is the last time you learned something new out of your comfort zone? Perhaps you bought a new cell phone, installed a new computer program, or adopted a new curriculum. What did you notice about yourself as you tried to learn to use the new material? Were you often frustrated or even angry? Did you need time to practice the new material more than once? Did you need someone who knew more than you and who would give you uncritical support? Was there a guidebook with clear directions?

Learning something new gives us the opportunity to reflect upon the challenges and fears our students face daily: the stress and threat of failure, peer or teacher criticism, material presented outside of student learning styles, and grades given before the material is mastered. In addition, if you are a student who often experiences failure, you may lack the self-confidence in your ability to master the new task.

CLASSROOMS THAT WELCOME STUDENTS

Therefore, students need classrooms where there is a strong sense of community, no fear of ridicule, and where the teacher not only cares about them but refuses to allow them to fail.

In your classroom, it might look like this:

You welcome each child, each day, into your classroom. You may do this with a hello at the door, using the student's name, or a variation of your own.

Consider this strategy: give each student a 4- × 6-inch index card. Have students print their names on the cards. Laminate them, if possible. Each day, lay the cards out in alphabetical order on a table inside the room. Students enter the room, pick up their cards, and greet you with a "Good morning, [teacher's name]" while shaking your hand. You reciprocate with a "Good morning, [student's name]" as you look into the student's eyes. After you enter the attendance, you recycle the cards to the table, ready for the next day. The young teacher who shared this strategy said that using this procedure has cut down on tardies, built classroom community, and allowed her to learn quickly a large number of students' names. Her students were ninth graders, but this strategy would work with students once they were old enough to recognize their names as well as with graduate students.

However you decide to welcome your students, this initial contact with them sets the tone for the class. Until you acknowledge the visibility of each student, you may find that particular students refuse to acknowledge your lesson. They may not care about what you are teaching until you demonstrate that you care about them.

Some classrooms use a strategy for students who are tardy that alleviates the stress and tension of the moment. There is a sign-in sheet right inside the classroom door and students sign in, marking the date and time. A local preschool uses this procedure beginning at age three, so our older kids can surely do this. It eliminates the dreaded question, "Why are you late?" Instead, the student can quietly enter the classroom and take his or her seat. Questions about tardies can happen at the end of class. This respects the learning, the teacher, and the student.

Write below how you welcome students to your class.

_____

_____

_____

If you are not satisfied with your procedure, devise a new positive welcoming ritual.

_____

_____

_____

BODY LANGUAGE

Once you have welcomed your students and connected with them, does your body language continue to connect with your students? Is your body language congruent with the words that come out of your mouth? A professor at UCLA, Albert Mehrabian (1990), did research on how people communicate their feelings and concluded that 38% of the meaning communicated is based on how it sounds—tone, volume, and speed. With that knowledge, think about your classroom tone. Is your tone appropriate and congruent with the words you say? To demonstrate the importance of tone, try this exercise: stand in front of a chair and pretend it is a dog. Pet it lovingly as you say something like this: "I hate you; you are evil and I don't want you." What would the dog do? Wag its tail and nuzzle up to you. Now kick the chair and scream these words in anger: "I love you, you sweet doggy." What would the dog do? Recoil in fear. So the tone conveys your message (and notice how much more difficult it is to say nice things in anger than to say mean things in a pleasant tone). Think about your students. Does your tone of voice often communicate displeasure, disappointment, or frustration as you say something such as "We are going to try this again"?

Ask a colleague to give you feedback on your tone of voice after he or she observes you teaching a challenging class.

Once you are convinced that your body language conveys an assertive, caring teacher, you may want to examine how you continue to build relationships throughout your school day. Students often come into class wound up or tired, certainly not focused on the lesson you are ready to teach. Yet the opening moments of class are tremendously important and offer countless opportunities to build classroom community and relationships. Think about your opening class procedure. How do you effectively begin your time with students?

GREETING YOUR STUDENTS

Have a colleague videotape your morning welcomes several days in a row so that you are unaware of it after the first few days. Do you lean into some students as you greet them and lean away from others? Is your smile more genuine with certain students? Do you joke around with some and not others? Do you tend to compliment the same students day after day? It is usually necessary to have outside eyes help with the monitoring of our body language. Body language is often unconscious, so we may not know what subtle cues we are sending to our students.

Describe your perception of the body language you use with your students.

_____

_____

_____

Think about a person you enjoy being around. Probably their body language is welcoming. Can you articulate what the person does to make you feel welcome? Describe the person's body language.

_____

_____

_____

What changes might you make in your body language?

_____

_____

_____

THE EMOTIONAL CLIMATE

Assess the vibrations of the class. This may make no sense to you, or you may be a person who knows exactly what this means. But look at each student. Look at their faces. Are they relaxed? Are they angry? Is the tenor of the class anticipatory? Is it belligerent? Assess the tenor of the class as a whole.

When presenting to a group of high school African American students on the day following the Rodney King verdict, I found the tenor anything but friendly. They had never met me, it was a Saturday morning, and they were there for some special job training. What did I do? I began by saying, "I bet the last thing you want is to be here with a middle-aged White lady who has come to tell you what to do." It worked. They laughed, and it allowed them to have a conversation about what they did want and what we needed to do that day.

If a fight just occurred in the hallway, students may come into class in a heightened emotional state and be physically unable to begin class work without transition time. Some students take much longer to transition than others. Consider allowing kids transition time. If you need quiet in your classroom immediately for behavior control, use writing in a journal as a transition. You can write a prompt on the board or overhead and have students respond to it in their journals. You can tie the prompt to the material to be studied in the class or not. You can choose several avenues for sharing: students share with a class buddy, students share with the whole class, students share with the teacher.

If you have a class that can talk without losing control, let them talk a minute while you take row, assess their feelings, and move throughout the classroom addressing students and making connections.

Level: Elementary/Middle/High

Some teachers have an opening routine that functions as a positive ritual. A ninth-grade teacher begins each class hour with a Venn diagram on her board. Over each section of the Venn diagram is a word from the ACT/SAT vocabulary lists. When students enter, they go to the board and write their names in the section of the Venn diagram that best describes them. For example, if the words are *loquacious* and *reticent*, they decide which terms best describe them and write their names in the appropriate space. The teacher then uses the words throughout the lesson that day and incorporates them into the word bank of the class. You can also use terms from your lesson. Let's say you are teaching about inlets and fjords. Write those two words on the sections of the Venn. Have students decide if they would rather be an inlet or a fjord and have them write in their journals why. This kicks up the exercise to the metaphorical level. This opening ritual sparks conversation centered on literacy and focuses the class as well as gives feedback to the teacher about how each student perceives himself or herself. If your class is particularly large, you might designate a row of students for each day of the week who might participate in the activity.

Level: Elementary/Middle/High

Begin class with a question. Ask the same question of each student in the class and give students an option to pass. The question can be related to the lesson or it can be personal, such as "Where would you most want to travel?" or "What is your favorite food?" Once again, the teacher receives feedback on the preferences of the students; the students learn something about each other; the students' focus changes to the classroom; each student's voice is valued; there isn't a right or wrong answer; and each student fulfills the teacher request, even if he or she says, "Pass."

Level: Elementary/Middle/High

An elementary teacher shared that she uses this questioning strategy each Monday in her fifth-grade class. One morning she was absent for a workshop, so before she left, she asked the substitute to perform the opening class ritual. The substitute did, yet when the teacher returned after lunch, her students asked to do the activity again because, they said, "We didn't get to do it with you!"

Level: Elementary/Middle/High

Another teacher gives her students a high five when they enter her room. In her absence, her students complained that the substitute did not do the high five. So the teacher made a picture of her hand on the school copy machine and taped it to her door. She told her students that if they wanted to, in her absence, they could high-five the copy of her hand on the door as they left the room. Many did.

You can use a simple signal that tells the students it is time to learn. For example, you might say, "Turn your brains on," as you forward snap your hand at brain level. Even though high school students may laugh when you do this, it is a cognitive reminder to focus on what is to come.

Relationships profoundly impact student readiness to learn (Sousa, 2001; Sylwester, 2000; Tomlinson, 2003). Whether they are English language learners, students from different cultures, students living in poverty, or students with learning disabilities, they need to know that teachers care about them (Haycock, 2001; Tomlinson, 2003). Below are several brain-friendly strategies to show your students you care and build relationships in your classroom.

Level: Elementary/Middle/High
Subject: Cross-curricular

- Select a difficult student and find a way to connect with him or her about something unrelated to school. Do this daily, outside of instructional time, until you see a change in the student's attitude toward you. This works! Try it over the next two weeks with one of your students. You may be amazed at his or her reaction to your caring conversation.
- Student as expert: learn what your students know and incorporate it into your lessons. For example, students at the high school level who live in the inner city were able to explain to students who live in the outer suburbs directions to many cultural and sporting centers. The suburban students were impressed with the urban students' knowledge of and ability to navigate the city.
- Try a "Friday Final Five" strategy: choose topics such as sports, music, hobbies, and special interests. Students who are experts on a topic sign up to do a Friday Final Five. They share their expertise with the class during the final five minutes of class on Fridays. They are allowed to bring preapproved props and demonstrate their expertise to their classmates.
- Snaps and taps: during class time, allow students to write positive comments about other students on slips of paper and drop them into a bowl. During the last minute of class, one student pulls out a slip of paper and reads the positive comment aloud to the class. The class gets five seconds to tap or snap. "Snap" consists of snapping the middle finger and the thumb modeling the beatnik applause; "tap" consists of drumming on the table or desks as loudly as they want—five seconds of controlled motor activity. Since one teacher began doing snaps and taps in her special education classroom, she reports that students are reserving their tapping for the end of class rather than tapping pencils or feet or hands throughout the class.

(Middle/High)

- Take students to an event that reflects their culture. Just accompanying students to a restaurant that serves food that reflects their culture builds relationships.
- Start a support group. See Chapter 17 for a model for a 4 A's group or start a chess club, a writing group, a book club, and so on.

(Continued)

(Continued)

- Give your challenging students a responsible position in your class. One seventh-grade girl challenged classroom management procedures, so I talked with her privately, complimenting her on her leadership skills, and put her in charge of seeing that the other students followed the procedures. She became a role model. When others began to talk during teacher instruction, she used peer pressure to positively coerce them to reengage with the lesson.
- Take some bananas and muffins and meet with a group of challenging students once a week for breakfast. Within six weeks, you should see a significant change in their behavior.

(Elementary/Middle/High)

- Use authentic projects to drive your curriculum and improve achievement (Sousa, 2001; Tate, 2003). You will build relationships with students if you conference with them during their work on authentic projects. For example, if they are interviewing veterans (see Chapter 15 on oral histories) and creating a book, you will build a classroom community of learners as well as improve your relationship with each individual learner.
- Attend extracurricular events in which your students participate.
- Create a library in your classroom by shopping at flea markets, book sales, and so on. Invite your students to take books they want to enjoy. Consider it a success, not a failure, if one doesn't come back.
- Do a "Walk and Talk." I volunteered to take a small group of boys with behavior issues on a daily walk during an extra class designated for alternative instruction. The boys enjoyed the outside, the walk and the talk, and their behavior issues diminished in not only my class but in the classes of the entire team.
- Use students' names in your examples when you teach. Personalize your lessons in as many ways as possible.
- Send postcards to students when you vacation. Bring back free mementos for your students.
- Create a classroom newsletter. Ask your district to provide professional development in PageMaker or some other computer program that allows you to easily produce a class newsletter. Include each student's voice. Send it home to parents to build parent-teacher relationships.
- Create a buzz book and include student and parent interests.
- Have students fill out information sheets at the beginning of the year so that you can have their interests on file. Try to include their interests into your instructional planning when relevant.
- Talk about your interests to your students. By sharing yourself with your students, you build relationships. My fifth-grade teacher taught each student to knit. We made scarves and mittens. What do I recall

from fifth grade? I remember it as my favorite year in elementary school because of this teacher. Teachers are interesting people, and you have much to share. Some teachers have shared with their students the following interests: elephants, motorcycles, sports, knitting, the books they read, travel, exotic flowers, hiking, and many, many more.

- Videotape yourself. Analyze your body language. Are you consistently friendly with all children? Do you try to build relationships with all children? Do you move away from some children and lean into others as you communicate about your interests to your students?

- Investigate TESA training. Teacher Expectations: Student Achievement looks at 15 teacher behaviors and how they inhibit or promote academic achievement.

- Do some reflection. If 20% of your students are into hip-hop and you can't stand it, how might that play out in your class? If you find some students' cultural norms, behaviors, or hidden rules repugnant, how might that be reflected in your body language as you interact with them? Note: Recently, in a workshop, a young teacher asked what he should do if he despised hip-hop. When asked what he thought he should do, he said respect the students and do his best. He answered his own question. We can't always bond with student interests, but we can respect that they might have different interests than we do.

- Establish journal buddies with your students.

- Get to know your students through their journal responses. Honestly respond to them. You will see a marked improvement in their behavior and academics using this strategy.

- Smile at your students and smile with them.

- Listen to your students.

Write your strategies for building relationships with your students.

_____

_____

_____

_____

_____

Hopefully, you found several strategies in this chapter to build relationships with your students. Once the relationship is in place, learning can flow. Chapter 11 begins the section in the book that outlines good instruction for all students, emphasizing the research that supports the academic success of diverse learners.

SUGGESTED READING

Gregory, Gayle, and Carolyn Chapman. 2002. *Differentiated Instructional Strategies: One Size Doesn't Fit All.*

Jensen, Eric. 1998. *Teaching With the Brain in Mind.*

Sousa, David. 2001. *How the Brain Learns.*

Sylwester, Robert. 2000. *A Biological Brain in a Cultural Classroom: Applying Biological Research to Classroom Management.*

Tomlinson, Carol Ann. 2003. *Fulfilling the Promise of the Differentiated Classroom: Strategies and Tools for Responsive Teaching.*

PART IV

Research-Based Teaching Strategies for Diverse Learners

11

Reaching Diverse Learners Through Strategic Instruction

Good instruction gets good results. Students learn. This chapter focuses on good instruction. During our first several years of teaching, many of us during the 1960s thought good instruction was all about the content—what we knew and imparted to the students. Most educators entering the field today know better. Thinking back, we realize that good instruction includes what we often neglected in those early years: making explicit the learning process, the instructional process, and the expectations. Did you ever say to students, as we did, "Just trust me, we'll get there"? We knew where we were going, but we didn't always fill our students in on the process. Not until we read research about learning styles (Silver, Strong, & Perini, 2000) did we understand how frustrated global learners, who need the big picture, or concrete learners, who need to know and control every detail, must have felt. The creative, off-the-wall students loved this kind of instruction because when they would ask if they could do a project "this way" or "that way" or a totally different way, we just got more and more excited, rather than saying no. This kind of teaching allowed for all kinds of thinking and learning, but students often did not understand the process explicitly in order to complete the task.

When the Madeline Hunter model reached our district in the 1980s, this changed. We were staff developed and evaluated, using her model. It made a tremendous difference in the way we taught. Later, the brain research yielded the work of David Sousa, Eric Jensen, and others, and we found why doing some of the things we did in class had worked, for example, humor and novelty.

One day I unintentionally employed novelty (Jensen, 1998; Sousa, 2001) while explicitly showing a class of high school seniors what hard work it is to write an essay. Having received Chapter 2 of my dissertation back from the professors for the sixth time, I was furious. A 30-page chapter was now 180 pages of draft. At the same time, my seniors were griping about their three-page essay assignment.

The next day, when they arrived for class, they found a room with all of the desks stacked in a corner and the floor covered with a quilt of 180 pages of draft writing. I had taped together my draft and laid it out on the floor. Students visually saw the revision process.

As our knowledge of teaching writing improved, we began using rubrics and supporting student writing. In our department we didn't redline student papers or take over their writing. The longer we taught, the more respect we gave student voices. The research of Donald Graves (1989) and Nancie Atwell (1998) helped us understand the importance of respecting the authentic voices of our students. Students began to write more authentically, for they trusted we would look for the hidden pearls in their writing and support their efforts in finding their stories.

USING THE RESEARCH

In recent years, the work of Robert Marzano (2004) informs our teaching. His book, *Building Background Knowledge for Academic Achievement*, explains and maps out what is needed to activate prior knowledge at increasingly deeper levels.

In addition, the differentiated instruction movement (Gregory & Chapman, 2002; Tomlinson, 2003) informs our teaching. Even though in the past we might have naturally differentiated instruction in several ways, we didn't really understand why (we did it mostly for variety). Now, books such as Marcia Tate's (2003) *Worksheets Don't Grow Dendrites: Instructional Strategies That Engage the Brain* make it much easier to include brain-compatible instruction within our differentiated instructional model.

Using a lesson design model, such as Wiggins and McTighe's (1998) *Understanding by Design*, has enriched the planning of our content instruction as we continue to improve our pedagogy in the classroom. McEwan (2002) writes that more than 24 lesson planning models exist, and skilled teachers select the model that best fits their content and learning outcomes, their students, and themselves. Our task is to find one that works for us.

ATTRIBUTES OF GOOD TEACHING

In the past decade, we have been blessed with a body of research and thoughtful practitioners that has made teaching more of a science, while our understanding of its art continues to expand.

Sometimes we teachers complain that teaching is hard work. It is! It is a profession that demands long hours, emotional give and take, and just about everything else one has to give on a job. It is not for the person searching for an easy living unless one plans to worksheet students to death as Mr. Ditto did in the film *Teachers*.

When good teaching occurs, you usually will find the following:

- Good relationships between students and the teacher
- High expectations for students
- The classroom bonding as a community of learners
- Good classroom management
- Lesson plan design based on research; the use of a model
- Goal setting for instruction
- Explicit instruction
- Graphic organizers
- Rubrics before instruction or completion of assignment
- Nonlinguistic organizers
- Assessment and accountability
- Goal setting for future achievement
- Humor
- Support from professional personnel such as counselors, special education instructors, nurses, administrators, and so on
- Good relationships with colleagues
- Valuable feedback from evaluators
- The belief that teaching is a profession, not just a job
- Professional development opportunities
- Opportunities to practice the discipline you teach—if you teach English, the opportunity to write for publication

Even though there are others not listed here, bottom line, when the teacher feels supported, the students feel supported and the learning occurs. When there is engagement between the teacher and the content, and students believe the teacher cares for them, the students will engage with the content and with the caring teacher.

Think about your teaching. What are your instructional strengths and challenges?

_____

_____

_____

_____

How does the research inform your instructional practice?

_____

_____

_____

_____

How would you like to improve your instructional practice?

_____

_____

_____

_____

Set three goals to improve your instructional practice.

_____

_____

_____

_____

STRATEGIES FOR
ACTIVATING METACOGNITION

In _What Every Teacher Should Know About Diverse Learners_, Donna Walker Tileston (2004) suggests five strategies for activating students' metacognitive system, getting them ready to learn.

1. Set goals and share them.

2. Show students how to set personal learning goals (Bishop, 2003).

3. Give students organizers, linguistic and nonlinguistic, as guides (Tate, 2004).

4. Teach students how to do self-talk.

5. Give students a rubric prior to learning (Tileston, 2004, pp. 50–51).

Diverse learners need to know the reasons they are doing the class work, and they need it tied to their personal experience. Over and over, this point is driven home in the literature about diverse learners (Marzano, 2003; Tileston, 2004). Setting goals, giving students organizational tools, teaching them self-talk, and giving them a rubric gives meaning to the instruction. Taking into account the differences of diversity in the classroom as you select content materials bridges the personal connection (Tileston, 2004).

CHECKLIST FOR GOOD INSTRUCTION

Our profession is rich with resources to help us become better at instruction. Think about your instruction as a continuum and each new instructional opportunity as another step on your path to a classroom of excellence. Consider using the following checklist for reflection.

_____ I know what I want students to learn (enduring understandings).

_____ I am using a design model for planning.

_____ I am using content materials, supplementary, if necessary, that match the ethnic diversity of my students.

_____ I understand that students learn in different ways and at different rates of time.

_____ I have built-in opportunities for additional time for students who need it.

_____ I am using instruction that matches student learning styles.

_____ I have students set learning goals for daily achievement as well as long-term goals.

_____ I have given students a rubric so they will know how they will be assessed.

_____ I am using differentiated instruction and brain-compatible instruction.

_____ I have specific strategies for activating background knowledge.

_____ Others

What insights did you gain from considering this checklist?

The following activities appeal to diverse learners and integrate the research-based strategies of cooperative group strategies, hands-on learning, and higher-level thinking skills.

Suggestions for Activities Across Disciplines for Diverse Learners Math/Science/Social Studies/Art/ Physical Education/Health/Family Consumer Science

- Math: Level—Elementary/Middle/High; Standard—Knowledge of mathematical terms.

  Students create a "Pictionary" of their assigned vocabulary words (Tate, 2003). Each student makes his/her own dictionary, complete with the word, an illustration of the word, and a definition in their own words. A local math teacher did this with great success, and he lets students use these dictionaries on their tests. He used the Frayer model as a guide for each page.

- Science: Level—Elementary/Middle/High; Standard—Characteristics of living organisms.

  Students choose an organ of the body and write a story in first person as if they were that body part. For example, if John chooses the liver, he writes as if his liver is telling the story. This allows students to incorporate biological functions of the organs into their stories while practicing creative writing skills. Students illustrate their organ story with illustrations and share with their classmates. Hang the final products in the classroom or in the school hallways.

- Science: Level—Middle/High; Standard—Processes of scientific inquiry.

  Teachers give the instructions for a lab to the students in their usual manner. They time the length of time it takes the students to begin the actual lab tasks. For the next lab, teachers give the instructions in a different manner. Now they give only one instruction at a time and wait for every student to comply. For example, "Take out your lab manuals." (Waits for all students to complete the task.) "Walk quietly to your student group." (Waits for all students to comply.) Teachers once again time how long it takes students to begin the actual lab tasks. They compare which method works best. Students with limited English skills will probably function better when teachers give one direction at a time;

(Continued)

(Continued)

and to the teachers' surprise, they may find that they save time by giving directions one at a time.

- Social Studies: Level—Elementary/Middle/High; Standard—Relationships of individuals to institutions and cultural traditions.

  Students keep first-person journals of the characters in their history books. For example, while studying the Civil War, one student will keep a first-person journal of President Lincoln, one will keep a first-person journal of Mary Todd, one will be a plantation owner, and so on. Allow students to choose the historical character they want; otherwise, you may find less than motivated students. When students complete their journals, let them create covers for them. A local middle school did this unit and made various kinds of imaginative covers from brown paper bags (burning the edges for effect), pieces of quilts, ties sewn together, and collages of various materials.

- Math: Level—Upper Elementary/Middle/High; Standard—Number sense.

  Students create raps to describe the functions of mathematics. For example, when doing a rap on reducing fractions, one student says his or her rap while the other students, in choral response, say, "Reduce! Reduce!" This provides participation by all students and allows students with limited English skills an opportunity to speak English in a non-threatening way.

- Science: Level—Elementary/Middle/High; Standard—Composition and structure of the universe; impact of human activity upon resources and the environment.

  Use video field trips. A local teacher has videotaped his summer excavation trips in Montana as well as his local trips to the Missouri woods and his nighttime observations with his telescope. He then shows these to his students, using them when they best fit the curriculum. This builds background knowledge in students and is one of the suggested strategies by Robert Marzano (2004) in his book *Building Background Knowledge for Academic Achievement*.

- Math: Level—Upper Elementary/Middle/High; Standard—Number sense.

  Use the statistics from sporting events to teach mathematics. Incorporate sporting events that are popular in the cultures of your diverse learners. For example, soccer (called "football" in most countries outside the United States), popular in many countries, basketball, baseball, and United States's football appeal to many diverse learners. Connecting to our students' lives and interests increases their interest in our instruction (Marzano, 2004).

- Math: Level—Middle/High; Standard—Application of mathematical operations in the workplace and other situations.

    Students bring in public transportation schedules. Students who use public transportation can teach those who don't use public transportation how to read the schedules. In a local classroom, some honor students received an important lesson when they had to be taught how to read the local bus schedule by the diverse learners who took the transportation each day.

- History/Social Studies: Level—Upper Elementary/Middle/High; Standard—Major elements of geographical study and analysis and their relationships to changes in society and environment.

    Students choose a country of interest. Using the Internet and library and other resources, they study this country for several weeks. They write a journal as a citizen of this country. They collect recipes from this country. They make a model of the topography of the country. They collect artifacts of the country. The class holds an International Night for families and staff, and each student occupies a table holding his or her project with foods for participants. One local middle school holds this event yearly, and it is packed with families. Administrators and teachers are sensitive to the economic realities of their students and provide what is needed for children in poverty to do the unit.

- Fine Arts: Level—Elementary/Middle/High; Standard—Interrelationships of visual and performing arts and the relationships of the arts to other disciplines.

    If you are a fine arts instructor, consider your expertise. You are the person who can give the core content area teachers invaluable suggestions about incorporating art and performance into their curriculum. Most of the activities in this book easily lend themselves to the inclusion of art and performance.

- Health/Physical Education: Level—Elementary/Middle/High; Standard—Principles and practices of physical and mental health.

    Students take surveys about their physical and mental health practices. They choose a topic of interest, such as physical exercise, good dietary habits, mental health, and so on. Students work in groups to investigate their topics, using the Internet and library resources. They prepare a panel presentation and present to the class.

- Family Consumer Science: Level—Middle/High; Standard—Methods used to assess health, reduce risk factors, and avoid high-risk behaviors.

    Students or teacher chooses groups. Students investigate and research a food group. They prepare foods from that group that research suggests supports good health. Students present their information in a panel format, followed by a meal of the food group. Don't forget to include the suggested benefits of herbs and spices.

This chapter outlined the learning process and offered numerous suggestions to improve pedagogy. It is not enough to stand in front of the classroom and spew out the content. Our students deserve strategies that scaffold their learning and support their achievement. Fortunately, the research on learning has informed our practice, and we now have a template for good instruction. Chapter 12 continues the dialogue on instruction, focusing on teaching diverse learners to love to read and write.

SUGGESTED READING

Marzano, Robert. 2004. *Building Background Knowledge for Academic Achievement.*

McEwan, Elaine K. 2002. *Ten Traits of Highly Effective Teachers: How to Hire, Coach, and Mentor Successful Teachers.*

Stone, Randi. 2002. *Best Practices for High School Classrooms: What Award-Winning Secondary Teachers Do.*

Tate, Marcia, L. 2003. *Worksheets Don't Grow Dendrites: Instructional Strategies That Engage the Brain.*

Tileston, Donna Walker. 2004. *What Every Teacher Should Know About Diverse Learners.*

Tomlinson, Carol Ann. 2003. *Fulfilling the Promise of the Differentiated Classroom.*

12

Inspiring Diverse Learners to Love Reading and Writing

How do we teach diverse learners to love to read and write? Students should love to read and write. Reading takes us to other worlds, offering us excitement, solace, understanding, and companionship. Writing gives us power—the power to influence and change our world, the means to ameliorate friendships through written communication, the tool to understand our inner selves. Yet, all too often, our students resist reading and writing. This chapter discusses ways to cause students to fall in love with reading and writing.

Do your students resist falling in love with reading and writing? Why? There are several reasons:

- They may have had teachers who weren't readers and writers themselves.
- They may be in schools where a culture of reading and writing is not valued.
- They may not see themselves in their assigned texts in schools.
- They may never be offered the opportunities to write about themselves and tell the most important story—their own.
- They may not know how to read or to write.

What can you do to motivate all of your students to love reading and writing? Reading is a complex, recursive thinking process (Fielding & Pearson, 1994; Ogle, cited in Tovani, 2000, p. 17), and successful readers use these strategies to navigate the process (Pearson et al., cited in Tovani, 2000, p. 17):

- They use existing knowledge to make sense of new information.
- They ask questions about the text before, during, and after reading.
- They draw inferences from the text.
- They monitor their comprehension.
- They use strategies when they don't comprehend.
- They decide what is important.
- They synthesize information to create new thinking.

Knowing that students need these strategies, what do you do to encourage your students to develop these skills and learn to love reading? For too many students, reading is just "eating" words with no time to savor them, thinking about the text, and connecting it to their world (Keene & Zimmermann, 1997). And for diverse learners, who may not find themselves represented in the required texts, this can be an even more formidable task.

TEXTS THAT REFLECT CULTURES

It is important for students to read texts that reflect their cultures and reflect them accurately. Students need to recognize stereotypes, either by omission or by caricature (Fountas & Pinnell, 2001). Finding ways for students to make connections to their own lives and to other texts can build motivation in the most stubborn of readers. For example, finding the "right" text for the unmotivated reader can open him or her to the world of reading. Hispanic students can perhaps find themselves reflected in books such as *Mother Goose on the Rio Grande* by Frances Alexander (1997) or *My Name Is Jorge on Both Sides of the River* by Jane Medina (1999). The Bluford Series has hooked scores of readers in our metropolitan area. These books are short, with compelling covers illustrated with African American adolescents, and the stories relate to young lives. You can buy them online at www.townsend press.com, and they are offered in a kit with a teacher's guide.

You can find additional books that teens enjoy in *I Hear America Reading* by Jim Burke (1999b). Burke lists books that teenage boys enjoy such as *Always Running* by Luis Rodriquez, *Enders Game* by Orson Scott Card, *The Things They Carried* by Tim O'Brien, and *Way Past Cool* by Jess Mowry, and he includes lists of books such as *Books for a Small Planet: A Multicultural-Intercultural Bibliography for Young English Language Learners* by Dorothy Brown and *500 Great Books for Girls: More Than 500 Books to Inspire Today's Girls and Tomorrow's Women* by Kathy Odean.

YOUR READING LIFE AND HISTORY

Finding that right book for each reader is an art and a skill that we continue to refine as we share our own love of reading with our students. Who we are as readers is important. Take the following survey to check your love of reading.

- Are you a reader?
- Do you love to read?
- Do you always carry a book with you?
- Do you read a daily newspaper?

- Do you know what books are on the list of bestsellers?
- Do your students see you reading?
- Do your students hear you talk about what you are reading?
- Is your voice passionate when you talk about reading?
- Are you expecting your students to do and love something for which you show no passion?
- Can we really ask another human being to do what we are unwilling to do?

Write a short reflection about what these questions say personally to you.

_____

_____

_____

_____

_____

_____

Think about reading in your life. Did your parents read to you? Was your childhood home filled with books? Did you observe your parents reading? What is the first book you read? What was your *favorite* childhood book?

Answering these questions can reveal just how important reading is to you. Do you think your students will think reading is more important than you think it is? Unless you are a voracious reader who speaks passionately about reading to your students, you may find that your students are less than passionate about reading.

Write your reading history in the space provided below.

_____

_____

_____

_____

_____

_____

_____

Let me share my story.

I grew up in a home where my mother read a story to my sisters and me each night at bedtime. I kept lots of children's books in my bedroom. I don't recall ever seeing my parents read a book, but both of my parents read the daily newspaper. On Sundays, my dad would read the funnies to me from the Sunday newspaper.

I remember learning to read in first grade. I remember practicing the letter sounds. I loved reading from the start. I checked out library books whenever I could, and I read every spare moment. During the summer, I would pride myself on reading a book a day. By fifth grade I was reading mysteries and historical fiction. I read the Nancy Drew series and remember them as my favorites for those middle years. By junior high I was reading biographies, and I remember my mother begging me to go "outside and play" instead of sitting inside on summer days reading a book.

In high school I began to read serious literature, and I was blessed to have an outstanding English teacher, Sister Francesca, for my last three years of high school English. She laughed often and loved literature. When I commented to her that I liked Robert Frost, she handed me a paperback copy of his poems. I still have it today. It has the price clearly marked on the front cover—35 cents. I continued to read for hours each day.

Needless to say, I became a good reader, and when I didn't know what major to declare when I began college, I chose the subject in which I had made an A— freshman honors English. I didn't grow up wanting to be an English teacher. Loving to read led me to that vocation.

My love of reading continues today. I am always reading several books. Usually I am reading a couple of nonfiction texts, one text of fiction, several magazines, a newspaper, and several periodicals. I tear articles out of newspapers, magazines, and periodicals weekly and store them in my categories of interest. Several of my friendships revolve around reading: we discuss and love books.

Books are my friends. You can show your students who search for companionship how books can be their friends too.

When you have a reading life that you passionately share with your students, you build the foundation for a classroom of readers.

How does that work? Try these strategies.

**Level: Elementary/Middle/HighSchool/Adult
Subject: Cross-curricular**

- Share daily with your students the book you are currently reading. You can do this during those empty last three minutes of class or as an opening positive ritual to begin each class day. Read a short passage to them. Do a think-aloud for your students. During the mid-1980s, researchers studied the merits of thinking out loud or "mental modeling" (Pearson, Rohler, Dole, & Duffy, 1992). When you model for students your invisible reading process, you empower them with reading strategies. Students who can think aloud about what is happening in their minds are better able to summarize information (Silven & Vauras, 1992). When you model aloud your thinking and the act of summarizing, you actively show students how to do it. As you read aloud, tell your students to ask questions about the book. Ask them to predict or infer about the plot based on what you share with them. Ask them to compare this book with others. (Elementary/Middle/High)

- Post your book list in the room along with theirs so that students can see what you are reading. Post yours near the door entrance or light switch. (Elementary/Middle/High)
- Take students to bookstores. If your school is close to a bookstore, you might do this during the school day. One teacher walks her high school students to the book store (10 minutes), lets them peruse (20), and walks back (10), all during their assigned English hour. Walking to and from the store gives the teacher an opportunity to interact informally with students and builds classroom community. (High—Elementary and Middle may require an aide or parents to accompany you.)
- Check out books from the local library. One middle school teacher checks out 100 books at a time. He keeps them on a cart in his classroom, and students use them for sustained silent reading (SSR). The local librarians now know him, and they suggest books and help him load them into his car each trip. (Elementary/Middle/High)
- Arrange for a storyteller to come to your class. Survey your parents. You probably have at least one parent who tells stories. Check your local cultural institutions for information on local storytellers. (Elementary/Middle)
- Ask an author to come to your class. Once again, check with your cultural institutions for local authors. Publishers usually have a list of authors who present. Check with your PTO or district to find a funding source to support author appearances. (Elementary/Middle/High)
- Make reading, writing, and thinking, not lecturing, the focal point of your classroom. Begin units with literally piles of books that cover your topic. Give students one class hour to peruse and find something that interests them to share at the end of class or the following day. This works especially well with poetry. Students read poems during the class hour, then find a poem they are willing to read to the class the following day. Students have an opportunity to hear 20 poems or more read by peers. This builds an interest in and acceptance for the study of poetry. This works with topics as diverse as dinosaurs (in elementary school), historical periods (in middle school), and universities (in high school). Try it with your discipline. (Elementary/Middle/High)
- Give books to students. Occasionally surprise a student with a book after he or she expresses an interest in the book or related topic. (Elementary/Middle/High)
- Have students order their own books from student book clubs. (Elementary/Middle/High)
- Allow students to choose some of the books you order for your class library. (Elementary/Middle/High)
- Be sure that your classroom books reflect all the students in your classroom. (Elementary/Middle/High)
- Make SSR an integral part of your instruction. (Elementary/Middle/High)

Imagine a classroom where all of your students love to read. What would it look like? What sounds would you hear or not hear? How might you create that classroom?

_____

_____

_____

_____

WRITING FORMALLY AND INFORMALLY

Many of us are readers, but we may not think of ourselves as writers, yet we are called upon to teach students to write. Do you eagerly anticipate teaching your students to write, and do they enjoy writing in your classroom, no matter what the subject or grade level?

If our students are to be effective writers, they need certain conditions. Donald Graves (cited in Burke, 2003) identifies seven conditions for effective writing: time, choice, response, demonstration, expectation, room structure, and evaluation. In addition, they need to feel comfortable in the classroom community in order to write and share and possibly even to feel motivated enough to try to write and share. Writing teachers also must feel passion about their own writing in order to instill the passion to write in their students (Tsujimoto, 2001).

Take this survey to check your love of writing.

- Are you a writer? Do you write letters, notes, grocery lists?
- Do you have regular e-mail correspondence with others?
- Do you keep a journal?
- Are you a secret poet?
- Do you keep scrapbooks with annotations for yourself or your children?
- Do you carry a notebook with you or in your car?
- Do your students see your writing?
- Do you write on the overhead or computer to demonstrate for your students?
- Do you give written feedback to students beyond correcting their errors?
- Do you communicate with your students through classroom journals?
- Do you contribute to a school newsletter?
- Do you send a classroom newsletter to parents?
- Is your voice passionate when you talk about writing?
- Have you submitted any written work for publication? This may be for a school publication, a newspaper, a journal, or other forms of publication.
- Are you expecting your students to love writing if you show no passion for the task?

Write a short reflection about what these questions say personally to you.

_____

_____

_____

_____

YOUR WRITING LIFE AND HISTORY

Think about writing in your life and recall your earliest memories. Did you write stories in elementary school? Did you receive positive feedback for your writing when you were young? Did your parents support your writing? Did your teachers provide multiple opportunities for you to write and share with others? Did you enter writing contests or perform your writing for others? Did you do well on college papers? What writing are you working on now?

Unless you are a teacher who writes and risks sharing your writing with your students, you may find your students less than enthusiastic about writing for you.

Trace your writing history.

_____

_____

_____

_____

_____

_____

Let me share my story.

I learned to write in early elementary school. My father was an accountant, and my mother, a homemaker, wrote copious lists of things to do in addition to weekly letters to relatives.

I remember writing no stories or creative pieces in elementary school, but by high school I was writing long letters to friends and keeping a diary. English classes in the early 1960s were mostly grammar and essay tests, and I do not remember writing a paper to be graded until freshman year in college. As an English major, I wrote numerous papers leading up to a thesis and dissertation. However, I never recall thinking of myself as a writer but rather as a teacher who wrote to learn. It wasn't until I was 40 years old that someone suggested I write an article based on my experience. At 46, I participated in a writers' workshop based on the Iowa Writing Project, and for the first time wrote creative pieces to share with others. Sharing personal stories with others altered the way I saw myself. For the first time, I valued my writing and felt I might have something to share. Until this day, believing that I am a writer is a scary thought. For me, writing is so much more personal and difficult than reading.

SELF-STRATEGY

One of the best ways to explore your writing life is to join a writing group. Find a small group of friends who want to meet regularly to write and share. You may decide to meet weekly or monthly. You may rotate locations, using each other's homes or meet at a local coffee shop. You may include food or simply write and share. Another way to explore your writing life is to keep a morning journal. Save those first precious waking moments for you. Putting your writing life on your calendar is one method of ensuring that you write regularly and flex your writing muscle.

When you write regularly and you passionately share your writing in your classroom, you build the foundation for a classroom of writers.

How does that work? Try these strategies:

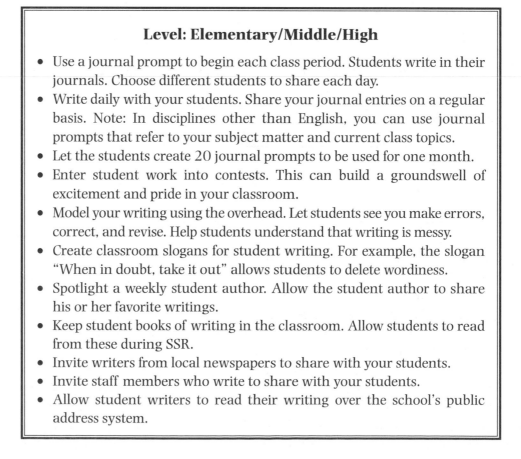

Level: Elementary/Middle/High

- Use a journal prompt to begin each class period. Students write in their journals. Choose different students to share each day.
- Write daily with your students. Share your journal entries on a regular basis. Note: In disciplines other than English, you can use journal prompts that refer to your subject matter and current class topics.
- Let the students create 20 journal prompts to be used for one month.
- Enter student work into contests. This can build a groundswell of excitement and pride in your classroom.
- Model your writing using the overhead. Let students see you make errors, correct, and revise. Help students understand that writing is messy.
- Create classroom slogans for student writing. For example, the slogan "When in doubt, take it out" allows students to delete wordiness.
- Spotlight a weekly student author. Allow the student author to share his or her favorite writings.
- Keep student books of writing in the classroom. Allow students to read from these during SSR.
- Invite writers from local newspapers to share with your students.
- Invite staff members who write to share with your students.
- Allow student writers to read their writing over the school's public address system.

- Schedule a Writers' Showcase monthly. The following is a model we developed in a high school that worked beautifully and continued to grow in numbers. Model: Use student lunch hours so as not to disrupt class time. During lunch, students who want to participate gather in a room where they are allowed to eat. Students sign up the week before the showcase with the teacher in charge. The teacher schedules the students, and students read their poems, stories, or pieces. The audience listens and gives positive feedback. Often, staff members join in and also share their writing. This is a *no-cost* method of building a writing culture in your school. Create your own model.
- Start a writers' club. Meet with students before or after school one day per week and let students write and share. Provide snacks, if appropriate.
- Pair your class with pen pals at a different school or even in a different country via satellite. You can build bridges through writing when students communicate with each other and discover their similarities, no matter where they live.
- Do a round-robin story. Have one student write a paragraph, then hand it to another student to write the next paragraph. Continue for as long as you want. Students usually like to write stories with their peers.
- Visit a school where students write often, display their writing, and win contests. Interview students and ask them what occurs in their school that supports their writing successes.
- Post written student work (but not work with errors or inflated grades). Lisa Delpit (1995) points out in *Other People's Children* that we do our students a disservice when we imply that the "product" is not important. In our society, students will be judged on the product. We must teach our students the "hidden codes" or rules of the product at hand; otherwise, our students of other cultures may believe that there are secrets being withheld from them and that the teacher is not teaching them what is necessary for them to succeed. As Lisa Delpit states: "Pretending that gatekeeping points don't exist is to ensure that many students will not pass through them" (p. 39).

Imagine a classroom where all your students love to write. What would it look like? What conversations would you hear? What would you see posted on the walls? Describe that classroom.

_____

_____

_____

_____

Decide which strategies you are willing to implement to create a classroom of readers and writers. List them below.

_____

_____

_____

_____

Teaching students to love to read and write creates an abundant classroom—one alive with literacy. Students rush in for SSR, anxious to delve into their books. They rush to the computers, anxious to continue writing their stories. Once again, when the writing and reading connects to the students' lives, literacy is alive with meaning.

To keep literacy alive, teachers can read aloud in their classrooms. The next chapter suggests ways to read aloud to students, engaging their attention and supporting their thinking.

SUGGESTED READING

Middle School Level

Atwell, Nancie. 1997. *In the Middle: Writing, Reading and Learning with Adolescents.*

High School Level

Burke, Jim. 1999. *The English Teacher's Companion: A Complete Guide to Classroom, Curriculum, and the Profession.*
Burke, Jim. 1999. *I Hear America Reading: Why We Read, What We Read.*

Elementary Level

Fountas, Irene C., and Gay Su Pinnell. 2001. *Guiding Readers and Writers, Grades 3–6: Teaching Comprehension, Genre, and Content Literacy.*
Graves, Donald H. 1989. *Experiment With Fiction.*

13

Improving
Reading Skills

Reading Aloud

Reading aloud builds better readers at all levels (Educational Research Service, 1999). It is an activity we can use in our classrooms to build a community of learners and help level the playing field for struggling readers. We find struggling readers at all levels, and students who experience failure at middle school have likely experienced failure as elementary school students. If they have been placed in remedial classes, they may spend a large amount of time engaged in passive activities such as worksheets (Allington & McGill-Franzen, 1990; Carbo, 1994). Even though basic skills instruction may be necessary and successful (Chall & Curtis, 1992), if it becomes the focus of the remedial class, students may lack time for reading that motivates them to love to read. Content area teachers often pose another challenge for the diverse learner. In a study of factors that hinder content reading programs, researchers found that the top hindrance was the belief that content teachers' responsibilities do not include reading instruction. Also, content area teachers often deemphasize readiness activities that teach reading skills (Ratekin, Simpson, Alvermann, & Dishner, 1985). Yet when content area teachers teach reading strategies, evidence suggests it makes a difference. These strategies include activating prior knowledge, building content vocabulary, and student-generated study guides (Santa, 1988). You can, however, use activities that increase your students' reading abilities, no matter what content you teach. One such activity is reading aloud to your students, whether they are elementary, middle, or high school students. Even though many secondary teachers view reading aloud as an activity not suited to adolescents as well as one that wastes valuable instructional time (Ecroyd, 1991), oral reading provides an opportunity for you to model reading, show your passion for your subject matter, and inspire students to get excited about the story (Educational Research Service, 1999). When you stretch beyond your textbook and find resources, such as primary sources, you can excite students in any content area.

Few strategies can transform the classroom as much as reading aloud to students. So simple, so elegant, yet so underused, reading aloud can produce students who love to be read to as well as students who love to read. Begin in the early years of school and in the early days of class. Reading aloud to students will change your classroom forever. Reading aloud is especially beneficial to your diverse learners and can motivate students to read on their own (Ecroyd, 1991). For those students who have never read an entire book, hearing a book read aloud from cover to cover offers them a sense of enjoyment of having completed a book (Educational Research Service, 1999).

MIDDLE SCHOOL

While teaching seventh grade, I donned a "wild and crazy" (remember comedian Steve Martin's early antics?) outfit and called myself "Book Woman." Halloween week I might wear a plastic vampire cape, witch's hat, and dark makeup and sweep into class on a broom; another week I might wear a beach hat, sunglasses, my Book Woman T-shirt (which the librarian gave me), and sandals. But each week the kids eagerly waited to see the transformation (and some weeks I was just too tired and told them that Book Woman wasn't coming that day). After making a grand entrance, Book Woman read aloud, in an exaggerated tone and accent, a passage and shared with students the latest, exciting book to be added to the class library. Upon hearing this strategy, a male teacher who teaches PE/health in another district transformed into "Health Man" to teach his weekly health topics.

Book Woman was just a gimmick; our real book work took place each day as I read to students, as students read to others, and as students read to themselves. We posted each student's book list on the classroom walls. These book lists carried weight; students would check to see what their friends were reading; they would check to see what their teacher was reading. Our conversation in the classroom centered around books.

The classroom was filled with hundreds of books—all kinds. Books were in the corners, on tables, on shelves. Books displayed on the chalk sill, making it a veritable display case, were changed weekly. Students would check the books on display and beg me to read them aloud.

I read daily to students! Daily reading works as a management strategy, encouraging students to find their seats and put their things away, so they can hear the continuation of a story.

How do you use reading aloud in your classroom?

_____

_____

_____

_____

How might you expand your reading-aloud strategies?

_____

_____

_____

_____

Consider these strategies:

- Level/Subject Area: Middle/High (Cross-curricular). Read aloud daily. Try the following books: _Holes_ (Sachar, 1998), _The House on Mango Street_ (Cisneros, 1989), _Seedfolks_ (Fleischman, 1997), and _Tears of a Tiger_ (Draper, 1994).
- Level/Subject Area: Elementary (Cross-curricular). Read a book aloud to the entire school. Each morning read five minutes of a book over the public address system. A middle school teacher read an entire book last year on a snow day when only a small number of children made it to school. They sat with their homeroom teachers while a book was read over the public address system. The principal said it was a resounding success.
- Level/Subject Area: Elementary/Middle (Cross-curricular). Create your own character who appears and discusses new and exciting books with your students.
- Level/Subject Area: Elementary/Middle/High (Cross-curricular). Read aloud to a small group of students. Auditory learners often prefer to hear a book rather than read it themselves. Because they were usually good readers and high achievers, I often gave them this option.
- Level/Subject Area: Elementary/Middle/High (Cross-curricular). Bring in real authors to read their works to the students, or if you teach in a place where that is not available, ask for volunteers among your parent or business population.

Think about your own reading past. Did your parents read aloud to you? Is that part of your positive reading history?

_____

_____

_____

In what ways can you create a positive reading history for your students by reading aloud to them?

_____

_____

_____

HIGH SCHOOL

Reading and Evaluating Fiction

During the first 21 years that I taught high school, I didn't use reading aloud as a daily strategy. During my last three years of teaching high school English, I changed my mind. Now, research is proving the importance of reading aloud (Carlson & Sherrill, 1988; Ecroyd, 1991; Educational Research Service, 1999; Krogness, 1995).

Also, I was teaching a diverse group of sophomores, and one of the students was a special education student who could barely read or write. Because of this, I was required to read aloud each of the five novels we studied that year. At the beginning of each novel, the students were offered several options for the reading of the novel. They could read silently to themselves, read aloud to a partner, or sit at the table where I read to the one student. To my surprise, the students with the highest grades chose to sit and listen to me read. After a bit of investigation into their learning styles, I found that they were auditory learners. They retained more of the novel by hearing it read, rather than by reading it themselves. This was a profound lesson for me, and it altered the way I taught literature.

Finally, in an elective class of seniors titled Contemporary World Literature, students were ready to graduate and did not want to settle into another novel. It was May, and we were to read Toni Morrison's _Song of Solomon_. Students largely ignored my minilessons, designed to interest them in the novel. In frustration, I asked a girl who was skipping class at least once a week to read aloud. She began and she changed the mood of the class. Students listened initially to her because she was popular and read well, but as the days went by, students listened because they could not wait to hear more of Toni Morrison's story. The girl's mother even called me to say that her daughter was more excited about reading this book aloud than about anything else she had done in classes her senior year.

Reading aloud offers a rich opportunity for brain-compatible instruction in the English classroom.

How might you rethink the way you use reading in your classroom?

_____

_____

_____

If you are a social studies teacher, a science teacher, or a teacher in another discipline, how might you use reading aloud as a successful teaching strategy?

_____

_____

_____

The following are strategies for content disciplines other than English:

- Level/Subject Area: Middle/High (Cross-curricular). Find articles about your subject matter in reputable periodicals and read them aloud to your students. These articles will contain excellent vocabulary words related to your subject matter.
- Level/Subject Area: Middle/High (Cross-curricular). Have the students read the articles aloud in groups. Ask the students to form questions about the articles.
- Level: Middle/High (Cross-curricular). Use reading aloud as an opportunity to unpack difficult texts, which occurs when you show your students a step-by-step process to approach a new piece of text and the reading strategies to use to comprehend the text.
- Level: Middle/High (Cross-curricular). Assign creative writing in your discipline. For example, when studying the cell in biology, students might assume the persona of one part of the cell and write a paragraph from that perspective. Students can read aloud their pieces and post them in the classroom. This not only builds community, but it also increases student interest in reading and in writing.

Think about how your professors in your subject area introduced the reading materials to you. Are there ways that you can better support your students when they confront new texts/articles in your subject area?

_____

_____

_____

_____

Reading aloud creates community and supports students in becoming better readers. It is heartwarming to walk by a teacher's door where a whole class is engaged with the book he or she is sharing with students. But what does an entire class of a reading and writing workshop look like as you pass by the door? In the next chapter, you will find descriptions of a reading and writing workshop implemented at four school sites: a middle school, a high school, a class in a prison, and a college classroom.

❖   ❖   ❖

SUGGESTED READING

Allen, Janet. 1999. _Words, Words, Words: Teaching Vocabulary in Grades 4–12._
Beers, Kylene. 2003. _When Kids Can't Read: What Teachers Can Do._
Fox, Mem. 2001. _Reading Magic: Why Reading Aloud to Our Children Will Change Their Lives Forever._

14

Building a Balanced Literacy Classroom

Reading and Writing Workshops

More than any other chapter, this chapter offers you a snapshot of how reading and writing instruction might appear in such diverse educational settings as a middle school, a high school, a college class, and a prison. You may be surprised by the commonalities. I was. Teaching in these four settings allowed me to see the research in action. We do know what creates good literacy classrooms, and this chapter spells out what good writers and readers need to be successful.

In 1991, I took a job teaching seventh-grade English in a diverse classroom. I had never taught seventh-grade students, and in fact, for the previous 14 years, I had only taught seniors in high school and adults. I naively thought it would be easy. I knew English, and I thought that was all it would take to be a successful English teacher of seventh-grade children.

How wrong I was! The first day was a disaster, and I soon found that these seventh graders were not impressed at all with having a new teacher who held a PhD in English. I had always believed that I had good classroom management, but within minutes, these adolescents convinced me otherwise.

I was desperate! I needed to find some pedagogy that would engage these children while maintaining the classroom atmosphere that I found acceptable. I found it in a reading and writing workshop.

A colleague introduced me to Nancie Atwell (1987), and I found my survival guide for the year in her book *In the Middle: Writing, Reading and Learning With Adolescents*. Donald Graves writes, in a foreword to Atwell's second edition (1997), that *In the Middle* is for the teacher with a "strong desire to help students make sense of their world through reading, writing, and sound thinking" (p. ix).

He adds that it also is for the teacher who commits to "grow in her own ability to write and read with students" (p. ix). One cannot occur without the other. This book changed the way I taught English, and it supported my students as they learned to love reading and writing. Actually, many of my students came to me already loving to read and to write because of their previous experiences, but Atwell's book allowed me to create a framework for a literacy-rich environment in my classroom.

Impressed by the results of using Atwell's workshop format, I extended the reading and writing workshop to three additional teaching assignments—the community college and the prison where I taught Composition 101 and 102 one night a week and then, two years later, to the high school classroom.

What follows is what it might look like in the classroom when you use a reading and writing workshop approach. For middle school and high school, consider arming yourself with Nancie Atwell's books, and for elementary school classrooms, try *Guiding Readers and Writers, Grades 3–6: Teaching Comprehension, Genre, and Content Literacy*. This book by Irene C. Fountas and Gay Su Pinnell (2001) is so comprehensive that it actually spells out day by day (for the first 20 days) what you do to include balanced literacy in your elementary school day. In addition, the differentiated instruction books by Gayle Gregory and Carolyn Chapman (2002) and others offer you a firm base for your planning.

INSIDE THE READING AND WRITING CLASSROOM

Imagine a group of individuals writing, some rather feverishly, some more relaxed, yet all intense, writing their stories, writing their lives. Imagine four very different settings: a seventh-grade class in an affluent county suburb, an English class for juniors and seniors at a suburban high school, a community college class in a middle-class neighborhood, and a prison class housed behind razor wire.

What do these four classes have in common?

These four classes share a writing and reading class environment that is almost identically structured, and they share the things that good writing classrooms provide: time, choice (Marzano, 2004), and positive response from teacher and peers (Caine & Caine, 1997).

Josh, a seventh-grade boy, can't wait to share his fourth story with the class. It's about a giant killer peanut.

Jenna, a senior girl, can't wait to share her story about the summer camp where she assisted a terminally ill adolescent in a wheelchair.

Janet, a 19-year-old student in my community college class, can't wait to share her first story with the class. It's about an event on her 16th birthday that changed her life forever—a rape.

Luke, a lifer in this maximum security prison for murder, can't wait to share his current story with the class. It's about the day his mother came to visit him in prison and died three hours later. (His story won first prize in a national fiction contest and was published in a magazine.) Donald Graves (1989) states that everything we tell is a fiction and a version of our own reality. This student turned his reality into fiction.

Each class sits in a circle as members share their stories. The seventh graders sit in a brightly lit, plant-filled, and colorful room, meticulously maintained.

The juniors/seniors sit in a classroom with bare walls on the lower level of an old four-story brick school building.

The college class chooses to sit in the park next to the class building, sharing coffee and rolls as they share their stories during their Saturday morning class.

The prison class sits in a stark concrete block room with no window and far too little ventilation with barely enough room between the desks to move.

The four groups work in similar ways.

Each student shares a story; members give positive, specific feedback—and all receive peer response. The writings are rich, revealing, and rewarding.

Because good writers learn from reading (Marzano, 2004), these four groups of students are required to read, read, read! The seventh graders read a book a week (or the equivalent of 150 pages), the juniors/seniors read four novels per semester class, the college class reads five classics a semester, and the prison class reads a classic a week. Each student is given a book list of authors from which to choose books. The list includes Toni Morrison, Alice Walker, and Barbara Kingsolver as well as William Faulkner, Ernest Hemingway, and F. Scott Fitzgerald and many young adolescent novels (YA novels) for the younger students.

Each week, time is spent discussing the students' reading. One student is responsible for leading the discussion or conducting a "booktalk." Then all students join in to discuss what they are reading.

THE PRISON CLASS

In the prison class, a discussion about John Steinbeck so inspired the men that the following classes became a Steinbeck seminar. Steinbeck especially appeals to these men who share a common denominator: poverty. The past experiences of these men caused them to connect to the lives of literary characters living in poverty, and this commonality inspired rich classroom conversation and writing.

Steinbeck's portrayal of those who suffer from hardships and poverty causes talk to erupt, and the men can't wait to search for copies of *The Grapes of Wrath, Tortilla Flat, Of Mice and Men*, and others. The booktalks become a powerful force that causes the group to bond men of different races and gangs who would not speak to each other outside this prison classroom. Both African American and White men talk and share ideas, not a common occurrence in an institution often rife with racial tensions.

Another popular book for these prison booktalks is *The Autobiography of Malcolm X*. Men who came into the class complaining that they did not like to read devoured this book. It is one of those books that motivates students to read above their grade level or reading ability. Try it with challenging middle school and high school students; it is a high-interest book that motivates students.

Mostly, I stay out of the booktalks. Once the men were hooked on books (and Steinbeck and *The Autobiography of Malcolm X* hooked them), they controlled the talk. One man, imprisoned in his teens, commented after reading

The Great Gatsby, "I don't know what I think about it. I think I'll read it again." What more could a teacher ask?

THE SEVENTH-GRADE CLASS

Choice is a must for seventh graders who believe that they must choose their own readings (at least some of the time) in order to prove their independence. Marzano's (2004) research on SSR programs stresses the need for students to have choice in their reading materials. When assigned *Across Five Aprils* to accompany their study of the Civil War, student responses varied tremendously.

Students reacted positively and negatively as they interacted with the literature, bringing to the work their own personal experiences and interpretations. One student said, "I have tried so hard to come up with something good to say about this book, but nothing comes to mind." Then she went on to write several paragraphs in her journal about her interpretation of the novel, proving that she had indeed interacted with the text and had learned from it. Rosenblatt (1995) stresses that students must interact with the texts they read, bringing something to the text as well as taking something from it, resulting in a transactional interaction. Students who are aware of this two-way relationship with the text are both better readers and comprehend more than those students who do not understand this powerful relationship. Her journal proved to be so cogent that it was accepted for publication in a national journal. Publication is a powerful motivator to the entire class, so consider any opportunity to publish your students' works both in the classroom and to a wider audience.

Students could honestly respond to the literature, and this created an open atmosphere that motivated students to read beyond their assigned texts. Both the students and I posted our book lists on the classroom walls and added a new book each week. Students eagerly checked to see what their peers and I had read and if the latest book had been recommended. The room was full of lists of recommendations. No student ever wondered what he or she could read; it was simply a matter of which book to read next.

On many Fridays, I came dressed as Book Woman, surprising the students with a crazy costume and a new book recommendation. (Note: I did *not* do this in the other classes.) After Book Woman disappeared, the rest of the class period was devoted to SSR. It was a wonderful, peaceful way to end the week with a room filled with high-energy seventh-grade students. This SSR also gave me time to keep up with my reading and to model reading for my students.

THE HIGH SCHOOL CLASS

The high school class had to cover the curriculum, consisting of many familiar classics: *The Great Gatsby, Death of a Salesman, The Scarlet Letter,* and others. Their writing assignments often revolved around their interactions with these texts, yet I offered options as often as possible. For example, after reading *Death of a Salesman*, students were allowed to write plays in cooperative groups and then perform them for the class. This was, by far, the most enjoyable writing assignment of the semester. Other options included the literary analysis (the most dreaded), the student writing a first-person journal as one of the characters in the story, creating a curriculum guide for the text, and inserting oneself into the text as a character and expanding the action to include the additional character.

After completing early drafts of their writing, the high school students enjoyed taking part in the Friday Buffet. This consisted of laying their anonymous papers out on a table on Fridays and using part of the class hour to read the papers of classmates. Stapled to each student paper was a colored sheet of paper on which the author asked a question of his or her readers. For example, a question might read, "Are there any parts of this that you think I should expand or explain better?" The student readers would read papers from the buffet and answer the question on the attached sheet of paper. At the end of the buffet time, students retrieved their papers and read the feedback from their peers. This feedback was then incorporated into next drafts, and the process continued until final drafts/publication when students shared their papers from the "author's chair." I also participated in this Friday Buffet, sharing my drafts of stories I was writing for a local university writing class, and as in the seventh-grade Friday SSR, this offered a calming and pleasant way to complete the academic week.

THE COLLEGE CLASS

The Saturday morning college class at a local community college was comprised mostly of working women earning minimum wage who wished to better their lives. (Consider reading *Nickel and Dimed* by Barbara Ehrenreich, 2001, for a comprehensive look at the working poor in the United States.)

Their reading history also had a common denominator—few had read any of the traditional or new classics or canon, and few were aware of the concerns of women from around the world.

As they read such novels as Mary Crow Dog's *Lakota Woman*, Alice Walker's *The Color Purple* and *Possessing the Secret of Joy*, these women were shocked to find what women suffered throughout global societies.

They kept weekly journals to describe their reading journeys (Atwell, 1997; Calkins, 1986; Macrorie, 1984). One student, after reading *Lakota Woman*, wrote that the book changed the way she looked at others. She wrote that she was determined not to become one of those Americans who thinks his or her way is the best way. Instead, she resolved to open her heart and mind to learn the ways of others.

The content of the novels that these students read opened their minds to worlds they would never have known had they not been required to pick up these books. We teachers have a responsibility to give our students provocative works of literature that expose them to many worlds. Our diverse learners need to see themselves reflected in the literature they read, yet today only 5% of the books being published are "culturally diverse." Culturally diverse texts accurately and respectfully portray people of different cultures and perspectives. This literature offers all students the opportunity to read and discuss issues of freedom, bias, justice, and equality and has the "power to humanize us and increase our sensitivity, tolerance, and compassion for people and other cultures" (Routman, 2000, p. 75B).

According to Galda (quoted in Routman (2000, pp. 74–75B), the culturally diverse literature about African Americans continues to increase, and there are some powerful Asian characters in the current literature; however, there are few accessible texts about Latino/a culture and a dearth of literature depicting our indigenous population. This continues to be a challenge for educators as we reach out to diverse learners.

WRITING IN THE FOUR CLASSES

Writing in the four classes was just as important as reading. Using Atwell's (1987) guidelines for writing proved successful for students at all levels. To these I would now add rubrics and an assessment component.

The guidelines for writing in the four classes are the following:

- Student choice of topics
- Personal conferences
- The teacher writes with students
- Peer response
- Specific, positive feedback
- Publication of student writing
- Student choice of reading
- Shared discussions about reading and writing
- Journal writing and sharing

JOURNAL RESPONSE

The journal was an integral part of all three writing classes (Atwell, 1997; Calkins, 1986; Macrorie, 1984). At the seventh-grade level, it functioned as a procedure to mark the beginning of each class as well as student writing. Students were asked to respond to questions or prompts written on the board. They then shared responses before they began their daily writing or reading tasks.

At the high school level, it functioned as a resource for future reading and writing ideas as well as the place where students interacted transactionally on paper about their books.

At the college level, students used their journals for reflection and processing. During the first classes of the semester, students would share their fears and doubts, and that sharing, and the ensuing discussion, would help build the class reading and writing community.

In all of the class discussions, one thing is paramount: the interaction that results from students confronting texts and each other. When students could construct their own meanings through their discussions, a community of readers and writers arose to support the discovery and learning of its members (Atwell, 1997).

THE TEACHER'S ROLE

So what is your role in a literacy classroom? The final component of this learning in a rich reading and writing environment is the teacher. Teachers, like musicians, are artists as well as practitioners (Palmer, 1998). The teacher who creates writing and reading magic in his or her classroom has a distinct voice, a timbre that resonates throughout the classroom. That teacher is not afraid of his or her own voice or the distinct voices of his or her students, whether those students are young or old, Black or White, rich or poor, innocent or guilty. Those teachers allow their students to take risks, and they also take risks.

Teachers must write in front of and with their students and share their failures and successes. Students also must be allowed to fail, but the teacher must offer the scaffolding and needed support that bolsters them to success. Consider allowing students to write and rewrite their papers over and over as often as they want in order to improve their grades. Think of sports. When basketball players begin to play the game, they do not perform perfect free shots over and over. It takes years of practice. When students begin writing, they must practice. Grading the practice shuts down the process. Instead, assess and give specific feedback, yet allow students to revise and rewrite until they believe it is the best they can do (Burke, 1999b). You can give points for completing the earlier drafts, but assign a letter grade only to the finished product. This creates a writing and reading environment that supports discovery and change, growth and development.

So what is the challenge for the teacher who wants to create a rich, balanced literacy program that supports reading and writing? Is it to impart a body of knowledge? Is it to get students to regurgitate "important" facts? Or is it to teach students to be reflective writers and readers who know how to gather information, process information, and synthesize information? The balanced literacy teacher must include all of the above. But if that teacher wants to get the very best from students, the teacher must create a climate of mutual trust and understanding where human beings can come together, no matter what their ages, to share their stories and writings of their lives within a common community (Gregory & Chapman, 2002).

Reflect upon these classrooms described above. How do they match what you already do? What aspects of the reading and writing workshops described above could you use in your instruction?

_____

_____

_____

_____

Following are some tools for your classroom:

Quick Self-Edit Ideas

- Use a good word processing program that includes a grammar and spell check. It will catch most of your errors.
- "Read to the Sky"—Go outside and read your piece aloud to the sky (okay, you can read inside and call it "Read to the Wall." Have students line up, facing the wall, and read their papers aloud, simultaneously). Listen for the parts you like and listen for the parts that sound awkward. Revise accordingly.
- Find the real beginning of your piece. If your piece contains more than 20 pages, consider cutting the first page and a half; if your piece contains fewer than 20 pages, consider cutting the first paragraph and a half. Read your piece aloud to a reader and ask him or her what he or she remembers; what is remembered may be the real beginning of your piece.
- Make people, not things, the subjects of your sentences.
- Eliminate passive voice and use active voice. Following the above often takes care of that. Example of passive voice: "The ball was thrown by Mike." Example of active voice: "Mike threw the ball."
- Eliminate linking verbs. Example with linking verb: "She was tired and fell asleep." Example without linking verb: "Tired, she fell asleep."
- Use active verbs to show the action. Do not put the action into adjectives or adverbs. Example with adverb: "John awkwardly walked across the room." Example without adverb: "John shuffled across the room."
- Cross out your prepositional phrases, then decide which ones you really need. Often they contain wordiness.

Other suggestions? Brainstorm.

REVISION

Donald Murray (1990) tells us that revision is "re-seeing" that allows us to see what we are writing and what it means. Consider these strategies for your students:

Suggestions for Revision

- Read your piece aloud several times.
- Put it away for several days.
- Have others read your piece and give you feedback.

- Change the point of view. If you used a third-person point of view, change it to first and see what happens. Or try the opposite.
- Begin at a different place in your writing.
- End before you think it is finished.
- Write past the present ending.
- Reorder time in your piece.
- Change the number of words. Take a 3,000-word story and rewrite it in 1,000 words.
- Tighten your language.

In this chapter, you have examined a reading and writing workshop model in practice. What were the successes? When using the workshop model, I found that behavior issues disappeared, except in rare cases, as students found their "flow" in the texts they wrote and read. Another outcome was the creation of a community of learners, at all levels. Students listened and respected each other's writings, and our caring community grew. Academic achievement improved overall as students improved their reading and writing skills. Students became readers and writers, and the school culture of academic literacy flourished. We built upon the academic literate environment by using project-oriented instruction throughout much of the year at the middle and high school levels. The next chapter focuses on specific literacy projects we used to further meet the needs of diverse learners.

❖ ❖ ❖

SUGGESTED READING

Atwell, Nancie. 1997. *In the Middle: Writing, Reading and Learning With Adolescents.*

Fountas, Irene C., and Gay Su Pinnell. 2001. *Guiding Readers and Writers, Grades 3–6: Teaching Comprehension, Genre, and Content Literacy.*

Gregory, Gayle, and Carolyn Chapman. 2002. *Differentiated Instructional Strategies: One Size Doesn't Fit All.*

15

Differentiating Instruction

This chapter presents six class projects that motivate students. These classroom literacy activities were used in heterogeneous classrooms with diverse learners. None of the activities was used in an honors class—important to mention, since educators are quick to point out that suggested activities might work with honors students but not with "regular" or "at-risk" students. Just the opposite is true: the more authentic and exciting the project, the more it might engage all students (Dornan, Rosen, & Wilson, 1997).

The interesting thing about these assignments, specifically the guidebook, the oral history, and the CliffsNotes, is that they incorporate far more class work aligned to state standards than the usual kinds of assignments we give in an English class. In other words, they are authentic assignments that cause students to develop and sharpen life skills. In *Educating Everybody's Children: Diverse Teaching Strategies for Diverse Learners* (Cole, 1995), Strategy 4.15 suggests practicing English by solving problems and doing work in cooperative groups. For when teachers organize work into heterogeneous, cooperative groups composed of native and nonnative speakers of English in order to give ELL children opportunities to practice their English in problem-solving situations, they learn more (p. 65). In addition, students were on task, motivated, and working cooperatively. With the guidebook and CliffsNotes projects, you can choose the groups or perhaps ask each student to choose one other student for a group, and then you fill in with the others. The groups for these projects were teacher chosen to ensure a mix of ethnic diversity, gender, ability levels, and diagnosed learning disorders.

EXAMPLE 1: GUIDEBOOK PROJECT

In 1994, armed with a new teaching assignment in an unfamiliar high school and assigned to teach ninth-grade nonhonors students, I realized that my students were also new to this building and perhaps as frightened as I was. How could we quickly learn about the staff, the hidden rules, and the physical places in this school setting? We decided to write a guidebook.

The kids thoroughly enjoyed this, and it relieved stress for both them and me. Following is a brief outline of one way to do this.

- Discuss with your students the need to create a guidebook to interest and motivate them.
- Ask them to select something or someone they want to interview, investigate, and write a chapter about for the guidebook.
- Make a list and post it of the student choices. Each student must write about a different person or topic. For example, one student, interested in basketball, interviewed the basketball coach. One student, interested in becoming a nurse, interviewed the school nurse.
- A student interested in art could draw a map of the campus and design the cover.
- Set up interview schedules.
- Students interview staff.
- Begin the writing process.
- Have students write drafts, read aloud to peers, peer edit, revise, proofread, and so on.
- Continue and complete the writing process.
- Do a final proofreading.
- Print and bind at a printing office or have your district print and bind the guidebook. Each student receives one book. In order to find money to pay for the printing and binding of the guidebooks, ask your department head, your administrators, your district literacy coordinator (assuming you have one), PTO, your local chamber of commerce, and so on. There is always money out there to support school projects. Finding it is the key.
- Have a Publication Day and invite parents.
- Do something especially nice for yourself the following weekend.

EXAMPLE 2: ORAL HISTORY PROJECT

The oral history project was a favorite of the heterogeneous, seventh-grade middle school students, and it built a new sense of community in the classroom. This was a major six-week project that used a balanced literacy and brain-compatible instructional approach to create a literacy product of which the students could be proud. There were *no* honors English classes at this middle school, so all levels were in these classes.

This is a condensed version of what occurred in the classroom:

- Experts from a local museum came to the classes to explain the oral history.
- Students read several oral histories.
- Students chose a person for their oral history and completed a letter/contract with that person.
- Students interviewed their chosen people, using cassette tapes.
- Students transcribed their interview, typing the transcription.
- Students shared their interviews in groups.
- Students made decisions about the use of the interview. They were to use the information from the interview to create an oral history. The oral history would not be a word-by-word transcription of the interview.
- Students began the creative revision process. They engaged in the entire writing process, peer editing, revising, editing, proofreading, and writing a final draft.
- Teacher did a final proof/edit. Students typed the final oral history.
- Students created a cover for their oral history.
- Students bound their oral history with a spiral bind on the school machine.
- Students created a class invitation for Oral History Day and gave it to their parents and the people they interviewed.
- Students planned the Oral History Day celebration, including typing the agenda for the celebration and student order for sharing.
- Everyone participated in the Oral History Day celebration. Once again, students participated as "real" writers in an authentic literacy assignment.

Students' oral histories brought tears to the eyes of the audience. One young man wrote about the elderly crossing guard who helped them across the busy avenue on the way home from school. It turned out that in the 1940s, this man was a railroad porter. He shared stories of historical segregation. He attended the celebration.

Another student shared her grandmother's story. She had to interview her grandmother by phone because she was ill and in another country and under house arrest, for she was the wife of the former ruler of the country. The grandmother died the night before the celebration, and as the young girl read her poem and her story about her grandmother, we were in tears.

Students wrote about their grandfathers, veterans of World War II. Students wrote about their fathers, veterans of Vietnam. Students wrote about their mothers, aunts, uncles, and others. Parents related how the oral history had caused their family to communicate in ways they had not previously done.

This is a powerful, authentic writing experience that allows students to enter the stories of real, living people as they share their stories in their own authentic voices. It's a win-win assignment.

Fortunately, there are several books available that detail how to do an oral history project in the classroom. Find one and use it for this project.

EXAMPLE 3: CLIFFSNOTES PROJECT

When students couldn't find CliffsNotes for Barbara Kingsolver's *The Bean Trees*, they gave me an idea for a writing assignment to accompany our study of this required text for high school sophomores in a nonhonors English class.

We formed cooperative learning groups and asked that each group create a CliffsNotes for *The Bean Trees*. We used a similar process to the ones outlined above.

This project required that each student read thoroughly the entire novel, digest it, and re-create it. Each student in the group selected a task. One student selected to format the book; one student wrote the introduction, consisting of the author information, list of characters, and brief overview; one student wrote the summaries and commentaries; one student wrote the analyses; and one student wrote the bibliography and selected reviews and critical articles. Students used a standard writing process to complete this project.

When the students concluded their CliffsNotes, the class selected the best example. They then composed a class letter and mailed it to CliffsNotes. In only weeks, the students received a wonderful letter congratulating them and telling them that their CliffsNotes was selected to be displayed at national conferences. The people at CliffsNotes also said that other teachers had already done what we thought was an original idea and had sent their students' work to them. But, they added, our students' work was the most authentic that they had received. Even though we had done a final edit/proof and required the students to do a final revision in order to have a perfectly correct final version, I did not insert my voice or alter the writing of my students. The publisher said that prior models they had received showed obvious teacher intervention. A good writing teacher must not co-opt her students' writing and turn it into her own teacher prose.

This project received acclaim and criticism. One community member wrote a letter saying that I was corrupting students with this assignment. He even appeared before the school board to complain. His children were not in the class.

On the other hand, CliffsNotes liked the results so much that they displayed the students' work at national conferences, and the city newspaper did a nice story with a picture of the students.

These class assignments included the following:

- Higher-level thinking
- Hard work for the students
- Hard work for the teacher
- Authentic writing: writing that students do in response to real-world issues or real tasks, such as writing an oral history or creating a CliffsNotes
- Balanced literacy: literacy activities that balance talking, listening, reading, and writing in the instruction
- Long-term goal planning
- Backward planning for student and teacher
- Cooperation among students
- Community building in the classroom, school, community

- Positive interaction with parents
- Student work for display
- Student work for publication
- Working like a real author
- Computer literacy
- National recognition
- Media recognition
- School board recognition (okay, that was negative. But later in the year, several of these same students were recognized for their award-winning writings)
- Fun/humor
- Intrinsic and extrinsic rewards

Write about a time when a favorite assignment, project, or lesson caused controversy. How did you handle it? What was the outcome?

_____

_____

_____

_____

_____

EXAMPLE 4: POETRY ASSIGNMENT PROJECT

This poetry format works for any class. You can use it at the middle school and high school level in English classes. It works at the elementary level too.

Students love poetry. And why not? Poetry is fun and begs for participation.

- Begin your poetry unit with choice, reading, and relaxation.
- Pile as many poetry books as you can gather from the school library, other classrooms, and your own library into the middle of the room.
- Move the desks to the outer edges of the room and invite the students to spend the hour looking through the poetry books, reading the poems that invited them, and then choosing one to share with the entire class. This ensures that each student becomes involved and invested in the poetry experience.
- Invite poets into your classroom. Place an invitation into the mailboxes of all your staff members and invite them to drop by on their planning periods to read a favorite poem to your class. You may find that there are poets among your staff. Some staff members may choose to read their own writing. When students see the football coach read a favorite poem, they understand that poetry is something to be shared by everyone.

- Immerse your students and yourself in poetry for several days or weeks. Begin the writing process. My favorite writing prompt for poetry is William Carlos Williams's poem "This Is Just to Say."
- Place that poem on an overhead and have students read it several times and discuss it.
- Model writing a poem for each class. Don't use one you have already written, because you do not want this to be a polished piece. You want to model for students how rough the initial jottings are so that they will model the same process as they write poetry.
- Laugh at your attempts. Invite students to suggest words. Play!
- Then ask students to write a poem that begins "This is just to say . . ."
- Have students write, share, revise, edit, proof, then type a final draft.
- Have a poetry party and invite teachers to read to the class. Invite another class. Invite parents or grandparents.
- Read the poems over the public address system. Display students' work.

EXAMPLE 5: YOU CAN BE IN A BOOK PROJECT

In addition to language arts, you can ask students to imagine what it would be like to live in different periods of history and then to write about it and share with the class.

Students become characters in the texts. This works for all ages, K–college. Ask students to choose a fictional text that they enjoy (or assign one you are studying in class). Tell them to write themselves into the action!

A group of sophomores used this strategy while reading *The Lord of the Flies* by William Golding. It was one of their favorite assignments. They keyboarded pages from the text and inserted themselves into the story. They made up dialogue for themselves, and it had to fit the overall style of the author.

This accomplished several things:

- Students who normally don't know how to begin a writing assignment had only to choose some pages and begin typing.
- Students programmed their brains with the style and syntax of a famous writer.
- Students were forced to pay attention to quotation marks and to use them correctly. This kind of exercise worked and was less painful to students than worksheets of exercises on quotation marks.
- Students had to extend the plot through their character yet match the intent of the author. This involved higher-level thinking skills.
- Students vicariously lived the adventures of the characters in famous books.
- Students enjoyed this assignment and enjoyed sharing it with their peers.

How can you grade this so you do not go crazy looking for the students' writing within the text of the novel?

- Students highlighted their prose.
- Students were required to write a stated number of words.
- Students were required to use quotation marks and other punctuation correctly.
- Students were required to match the syntax and the writing style of the author.
- Students were graded on completion of the assignment, creativity, and correctness.

EXAMPLE 6: THEME BOOKS PROJECT

This literacy activity is appropriate for elementary and middle school students. You can try it with high school students in a creative writing class. Once again, students created a class book, but this time, they wrote genre fictional stories. One group of students wrote detective stories, another group wrote mystery stories, another group wrote romance stories. Also, students who enjoyed art drew the covers, and the writing process followed the one previously discussed.

Students were expected to write fictional stories in their genre of choice that were a minimum of three typed pages.

Since we did not make copies of these for each student, we simply bound their final typed stories into books with a cover on a machine that the school owned.

These books became part of the library in the middle school classroom. This library consisted of hundreds of books scoured from garage sales, used bookstores, book order clubs, and student writing. Students *always* want to read their own writing, so on Fridays when they participated in SSR, they often chose a theme book to read. This settled them into reading, since students are interested in what their peers have written.

❖   ❖   ❖

These six projects offer opportunities for diverse learners to interact with their classmates while they engage in rigorous, higher-level academic work. Each project is aligned with multiple standards and can be adjusted to meet your students' needs. These projects also produce work that you can keep for years to use as models for future students, and in addition, the projects can become part of your in-class library and provide highly motivating reading materials for SSR.

In the next chapter, you will find multidisciplinary academic experiences that appeal to diverse learners and support their academic achievement.

16

Multidisciplinary Experiences

The multidisciplinary experiences described in this chapter offer suggestions for reaching diverse learners in our schools. Some took place outside the classroom and others were extensions of the classroom, but each experience offered students an opportunity to achieve.

What is academic achievement? It differs, depending upon whom you ask. Certainly, standardized test scores offer one measure of academic achievement. Teachers' grade books offer another. Yet another is the personal story, or anecdote. These testimonies of academic achievement can be gathered in many ways. One way to document academic achievement is through the use of an academic achievement journal. This is similar to a personal journal, for it documents our life's work. It is also a wonderful document to build classroom community.

There is no prescribed way to keep a journal, and there are several books in the marketplace that share journal strategies. A popular one is Mary Louise Holly's (1989) *Writing to Grow: Keeping a Personal-Professional Journal.* You can simply record stories from your own classroom or those that others share with you. The stories that follow describe authentic academic experiences that various educators have used with their students. Perhaps one will work with your students or spark an idea within you as you create your own.

USING PERSONAL WRITING TO INCREASE ACHIEVEMENT

Level: High

Subject: Language Arts/Multidisciplinary

SOURCE: Veljkovic and Schwartz (Eds.). (2001). *Writing From the Heart: Young People Share Their Wisdom: Best of the Laws of Life Essay Contest*, Vol. 1.

It's long been a personal belief that the more people have experienced in life, the more they have to say in writing. So, rather than searching out the honor students, a writing teacher might mine for writing gold among those in life's most troubled situations. Therefore, when an opportunity to pilot an essay contest arose in spring of 2000, sponsored by the local Character Education group, another teacher and I jumped on it. We introduced The Laws of Life Essay Contest at Covenant House, a shelter that offers services to young adults 17 to 21 years of age who have dropped out of high school. These students lived on the street and came to this day shelter to earn a GED. Contrary to popular stereotypes, these students were excited about writing their stories. This is the process we used: first, the students read samples of former winners and discussed them. Then the students talked about their own lives. Some students began to draft essays. Others needed more talk as a step to writing their drafts.

The following week (we worked with students once a week), students who had begun drafts read those to the class. The class listened and gave positive comments. Others began to write. The students worked on their essays for the next few weeks. We listened and asked questions that would expand the students' thinking. The students continued to read their essays to the class and comment on them.

Weeks later, the students handed in their final essays, and a panel used a rubric to judge them. The winner was selected, and the other essays were ranked and given individual awards based on the strength of each essay, such as "Best Descriptive Writing" or "Most Original Story" or "Best Character Development." In this way, each participant received recognition for his or her special writing strength.

A luncheon was held with special guests such as community leaders, and each spoke about the power of the essays and complimented the students on their writing and commitment. The winner, Kevin, was announced, and the other students were acknowledged. The students read their essays and received recognition for their hard work and persistence. Kevin's essay was selected to be published in *Writing From the Heart*. There were approximately 65,000 essay entries, and Kevin's was one of 62 to be published in the book.

The entire experience exemplified character education at its best. The students took an inward journey to examine who they were and what mattered to them, and then they expressed it in written form and shared it with an audience. The Laws of Life Essay Contest offers a positive format for adolescents to examine their codes of ethics and to develop laws of life to guide their lives. This is one of the many ways that educators can offer authentic academic experiences for their diverse students.

BOOKS THAT MOTIVATE STUDENTS

Level: Middle/High

Subject: Language Arts

SOURCE: Thornton (1995). *The Ditchdigger's Daughters: A Black Family's Astonishing Success Story.*

This inspirational book by Yvonne S. Thornton, MD, produced academic achievement in the classroom. First, I showed the movie based on Dr. Thornton's life to each of my classes. I then invited them (assigned) to write an essay for a contest that Yvonne Thornton was sponsoring. In the essay they had to detail their own struggles as adolescents. My students, White, Asian, and African American, wrote their authentic stories and submitted them to the essay contest. There were thousands of entries, and nine of the students were among the finalists. The finalists were invited to appear on a local cable television show and read their essays.

A month later, one student, an African American senior girl, received a personal letter from Yvonne Thornton. In the letter, Dr. Thornton wrote, "Your essay was excellent. I know that you did not win the essay contest, but if I were judging it, your essay would have been the grand prize winner." A copy of this letter is in the academic achievement journal of the class. What a treasure!

Students academically achieved in this activity. They wrote outstanding authentic essays that spoke to others. A favorite achievement anecdote throughout this entire process was Nick's achievement. He became so engrossed in this essay activity that he conferenced and revised and rewrote his essay 17 times. This was an African American male, in his junior year, who was determined to send a perfect paper to this contest. In the past, he had been a C/B student, but he accepted nothing short of perfection in writing this assignment. A year later, after Nick's first year of college, he returned to high school and told me he now kept the library doors open at night studying. This young man had evolved into a serious college student who was now tutoring others! Perhaps developing the work ethic to revise and rewrite his paper 17 times contributed to that academic growth.

This was not nearly as arduous as it sounds. Some of the 17 rewrites consisted of correcting one or two errors; some were more extensive. Nick and I also developed a close professional relationship because of this revision process. He would run to me with his essay; I would look it over, check errors, and he would run back to a computer. It was done in the spirit of success.

There are teachers who do not allow students to rewrite again and again until the paper is perfect, but you might consider allowing students to rewrite as many times as they wish. Once again, this is not as arduous as it sounds. Often, students choose not to rewrite and take a less desirable grade. For those students who choose to rewrite, simply place their former paper next to the revision and quickly skim the newer version to ensure that the student had revised/edited correctly. The few minutes it takes to do this are far outweighed by the product the student produces.

This assignment showcased the academic potential of diverse learners and elicited powerful student testimonies to the power of using one's authentic voice in writing. When students can use their authentic voices, they will engage with content. The above assignment offered that opportunity. All but two students did the assignment. These two students told me they could not relate to the assignment, and they were assigned an alternative. You may not agree with that and believe that every student should have to do the assignment. However, students will have many opportunities in school to do things they do not want to do; therefore, giving alternative assignments when it involves writing from the heart and mind offers students the opportunity to produce the most authentic pieces.

CONTESTS TO SHOWCASE ACHIEVEMENT

Level: Elementary/Middle/High

Subject: Cross-curricular

Submitting students' writing to essay contests is an incredible motivator. Students feel special when their work is submitted, and they work harder to improve their writing. If you have not done this before, consider it. You do not have to be a terribly organized person; you just need a system.

Look for contests in student magazines or writing magazines, such as *Poets and Writers*, at your local bookstore. One win will hook your students! You can always begin with an in-house contest to ensure a win.

Consider starting a writing club that meets weekly. Even a 20-minute block of time in your classroom before school works. Invite at-risk diverse learners. All they can say is no, and most likely, they will be pleased by your invitation, which signals to them that you believe they can write well enough to win contests.

The weekly meetings give you and the students time to share their writing, which is the best motivator for other students, and it also gives you time to complete the logistics of submission. Find a student who is really organized who will handle much of this work.

When students win, make sure their names are read over the public address system to the entire school. You will find that success breeds success and winning is contagious. More and more students will want to join your group.

One national contest a local high school writing club entered focused on inner-city students' lives. They submitted six personal stories from males who lived in the inner-city of St. Louis and were bused to this school as part of the desegregation program. A woman in charge of the contest called from Houston to tell me that they had the winning stories. She then asked, "Do all of your students write this well?" "Yes, they do," was my reply. When children are invited to use their authentic voices and given the support that they need, they do achieve.

In another incident, there was a notice of a book to be published about African American adolescent girls' stories. I remembered a girl's story I had heard in a class I had recently observed. I called the teacher and told her about it. The girl had to get her mother's permission to submit her story. That was not an easy task but was finally accomplished. Doing these things is not always a snap. It takes hard work and extra effort, but this teacher was willing to do it. They sent in the story. The girl was notified that it would be published as a story in this book. Recently, she was invited to read her story at a public book signing when the author was in St. Louis. Will that experience make that girl believe that she is a writer? Yes!

And this is why you might choose to do the messy work to submit your students' stories. Students begin to see themselves as real authors of their lives. Other teachers see them as winners. And they are.

Once you enter the contest circuit, you will receive all kinds of contest information. But one place where your students can submit is *Teen Ink*, a publication written by teens. You can contact them at *www.TeenInk.com.* There are contests and competitions in all disciplines, and getting students involved in them increases student interest and creates authentic work.

If you create ways to make your assignments authentic (meaning they write for real audiences and real situations, such as a contest or a newspaper editorial) using authentic student voices, you will find students engaged and academically achieving. Students want to achieve, and it is up to us to offer them opportunities for academic achievement.

USING PROFESSIONAL DEVELOPMENT TO BOLSTER ACADEMIC ACHIEVEMENT

Another avenue to ensure academic achievement for diverse learners is professional development for their teachers. Consider a "reading institute" where teachers gather together for a week during the summer to examine novels that appeal to diverse learners. A good text to use to gain an understanding for the necessity of using multicultural authors is *Multiple Voices, Multiple Texts: Reading in the Secondary Content Areas* by Reade Dornan, Lois Matz Rosen, and Marilyn Wilson (1997). Along with reading this text, consider YA novels and adult novels by diverse authors.

One success story of an institute held in this area was the study of Ntozake Shange's (1985) novel *Betsey Brown*. Shange writes about St. Louis in the late 1950s, the years that school integration took place in the city. Reading the novel, White teachers and African American teachers found common ground to discuss the impact of the civil rights movement on their city and their lives. Teachers revisited their city's neighborhoods through the reading of this text and found inspiration in the story of 13-year-old Betsey Brown.

Why not use literature that already connects the reader to the text, such as a book set in your hometown? Too often, we ignore what lies beneath our noses to seek out esoteric texts that say little to our children. One might assume that *Betsey Brown* is taught in every school in Missouri, but it is not. If we want diverse learners to achieve academically, they must see themselves in the content, at least some of the time, and this novel accomplishes that.

In addition to the text, there are several readily available supplementary materials for teachers who do not enjoy creating their own. Picador USA has a

Teacher's Guide for Betsey Brown, ISBN 0–312–28190–0. You can email your request to *academic@hholt.com*; fax to 212–645–2610; or mail to Holtzbrinck Academic Marketing, 115 West 18th Street, 6th floor, New York, NY 10011. Another guide is available in *Literature of Migration and Immigration: An Anthology of Curriculum Guides for Novels, Short Stories, Poetry, Biography and Drama*, which is available by calling the International Education Consortium at 314–692–9701.

REACHING OUT AND TOUCHING THE HEARTS OF PARENTS

Level: Elementary/Middle/High

Subject: Cross-curricular

A new teacher in the St. Louis Public Schools system shared a recent activity that she assigned. She told her eighth-grade students to go home and say to a parent or guardian, "How was your day?" The students thought the assignment was corny and complained, yet the next day, as they came into class, they beamed. She sat them in a circle and asked each student to share the experience. They excitedly shared the pleasant responses they had received from parents, two students remarking that their mothers had cried when they asked them about their day. What a powerful story of authentic voice! From that beginning, this teacher built community and a relationship with parents by assigning similar weekly assignments.

The following week she asked them to ask their parents if they could get them a drink of water or a soda. Once again, students balked; once again the stories were heartrending. The elegance and simplicity of these assignments set the stage for whole-class discussions, writing assignments based on the experiences, and community building among the teacher/students/parents.

This teacher built an authentic community based on sharing and caring, and parents called her to thank her for the assignments. Too often educators complain that parents are not involved or that they cannot contact parents, yet parents called this teacher who built a positive relationship with her students and their parents with a simple weekly assignment. Her clear and direct classroom instruction, entrenched within a framework of high teacher expectations and caring, supported all the students' learning.

ACADEMIC SUPPORT PROGRAMS

Level: Elementary/Middle/High

Many schools, universities, public agencies, and churches are supporting students' academic achievement through tutoring and leadership programs. You can find out about these by calling local agencies, school districts, and churches. Afterschool tutoring is invaluable in supporting the academic achievement of all children.

One middle school uses university students as tutors for their afterschool program. The university students volunteer, and the middle school students have both a mentor and a tutor. It is a win-win situation.

A high school has begun a mentoring program where the African American high school students travel weekly to two elementary schools in the district to mentor the fifth-grade African American students. The students volunteer their time, and the feedback is tremendous. An unexpected positive effect has been the improvement in the academic achievement of the high school students. They said they had to do better in order to be good examples for their mentees.

These are a few examples of educators who have nurtured their ideas to fruition through hard work and determination. We continue to create innovative experiences for diverse learners so that they can compete on a more level playing field and academically achieve. Break out your academic journal and jot down your ideas!

In the next chapter, you will read about a model for a student support group that is ongoing and focuses on academic achievement.

17

Sponsoring Academic Student Support Groups

Have you considered sponsoring a student group in your school setting? This chapter outlines one kind of student group: an academic support group for high school students. Researching the work of Banks (1994), Kunjufu (1988), and others, my colleagues and I organized an academic "club" at a high school that met weekly to support student achievement. If this idea appeals to you, you may want to research several models and then modify one and make it your own.

We proposed a model for a school club that would give external rewards to high school girls for their improved academic achievement. We received a district grant to fund the club following a study of the academic achievement gap between African American students and other students in the high school. The sponsors' goal was for the girls to make A's, so we created a name that included A's: The African American Academic Achievement Club (AAAA), or the 4 A's.

After receiving the grant, we invited all the African American high school girls to join. During the previous year, I had developed a relationship with five girls with whom I met weekly. Each Tuesday morning they met for 20 minutes before the first class of the day. Mainly, they knew they could count on me to be there, and if they ran into trouble at school, they knew they could come to me for support. These girls were the first to join, so they helped put up flyers throughout the school, announcing the new academic achievement club. Just seeing the flyers with "African American" and "Academic Achievement" on the same poster prompted some educators to make positive comments to the sponsors about the idea of the group.

The girls met weekly after school for approximately 30 minutes, and those who could not make the afterschool meetings met for 20 minutes before school in one sponsor's room. The focus was solely on improving their grades.

At the end of the first quarter of the school year, there was dramatic improvement in the girls' grades. No girl's grade had fallen, and most had significant improvement in their overall grade point average. The improvement continued throughout the year, and more and more girls joined the club. By the end of the year, nearly every African American girl in the school was a member.

A club for the boys also existed, and its model was based on a coaching model where the boys met in the sponsor's room each morning and huddled and set goals, much like players on a team. This group was called the American Black Achievers (ABA). Because of the expertise of the male sponsor, he used a model that was a better fit for the boys.

Each sponsor has different strengths, and each club has different strengths. The sponsors stressed academics, because they believed that if the girls began making B and A averages, they would begin to see themselves differently and the staff would view them differently. School behaviors would change—if they had been previously negative—when the girls began to experience academic success.

We explicitly taught and modeled what the girls had to do if they wanted to make B's and A's in the highly competitive, college prep school they found themselves. Most of these girls were taking part in the St. Louis Voluntary Desegregation Program, and they lived in the city of St. Louis. They traveled daily to this affluent district where resident students had years of sibling models, parents often had attended Ivy League schools, and resources were available to support most of their educational needs, including such things as weekly tutors to organize them, Koman math, ACT/SAT prep classes, and so on.

On the other hand, these girls needed to learn the hidden rules of this district, choose the best course of study, learn how to study most effectively, develop relationships with staff and students who could support their efforts, and withstand negative peer pressure. They were told that they needed to do approximately three hours of homework a night as well as eliminating most, if not all, phone calls and television during the week. The club brought in speakers, role models, other teachers, and anyone else who would encourage the girls to succeed. The girls ran the meetings and had individual responsibilities within the club; they did the attendance and much of the paperwork—it was their club.

At the end of the first semester, a television personality came to the awards ceremony to speak to the club and to distribute the rewards to the girls. She posed for a picture with each girl. The superintendent, the assistant superintendent, the principal, and the assistant principal attended, showing the girls and the staff that this club was important. A poignant moment occurred when a Black parent said that this was the first time she had come to the school for something positive rather than punitive regarding her child. The parents were so proud and turned out in large numbers. Teachers who had complained that Black parents didn't come to school functions now saw them proudly attending a celebratory function for their children. Eventually the club dropped its use of external rewards, and the girls continued because they wanted the support and camaraderie that the club offered them.

After the first semester, teachers began commenting about the "improved attitudes" of the "Black girls." These comments, along with proof of the improved grade point averages and the girls' attitudes toward schoolwork, made this club a success.

The 4 A's Club model can improve student achievement and change beliefs about student abilities. The model can function also as a staff development tool, because it forces staff to confront their attitudes about minority achievement, and, hopefully, to examine teaching practices. The club can and does work for the following reasons:

- It has a single focus—academic achievement.
- It offers concrete rewards in its first year for academic achievement.
- It meets weekly or more often.
- It teaches students how to study.
- It teaches students the hidden rules of the school culture.
- It teaches students the expectations that staff has for honor roll students.
- It reinforces academic achievement with ceremony and recognition.
- It continually reinforces participants' perceptions of themselves as academic achievers.
- It stresses to its participants that they will attend college and offers college visits.
- It offers tutorial assistance and other necessary support for participants to achieve academic excellence.
- It evolves differently in each setting, depending upon its sponsors and members.
- It receives support for its sponsors through staff support and networking.
- It has sponsors who are willing to take risks while risking the criticism of their colleagues.
- It has sponsors who are willing to make mistakes, learn from the students, and grow professionally.

An academic achievement group, such as the 4 A's Club, is but one strategy to improve the academic achievement of diverse learners, but it is a powerful strategy because it can change belief systems. It says to diverse learners that, yes, they are capable and they can achieve academically, and it says to the staff that, yes, these students are capable and they can achieve academically.

How might an academic achievement group work in your school setting?

_____

_____

_____

What steps can you take to create a student support group in your school?

_____

_____

_____

_____

Ultimately, our diverse learners must learn the hidden rules of academic success. Hopefully, in the chapters throughout this book, you have found strategies to teach these hidden rules to diverse learners.

❖ ❖ ❖

SUGGESTED READING

Peters, Stephen G. 2001. _Inspired to Learn: Why We Must Give Children Hope._
Wynn, Mychal. 1992. _Empowering African-American Males to Succeed: A Ten-Step Approach for Parents and Teachers._

Selected Bibliography

Adams, J. Q., & Strother-Adams, Pearlie. (2001). *Dealing with diversity.* Dubuque, IA: Kendall/Hunt.

Alexander, Frances. (1997). *Mother Goose on the Rio Grande.* Chicago: Passport Books.

Allen, Janet. (1999). *Words, words words: Teaching vocabulary in grades 4–12.* York, ME: Stenhouse.

Allen, Richard. (2002). *Impact teaching.* New York: Allyn & Bacon.

Allington, Richard L., & McGill-Franzen, Anne. (1990). Children with reading problems: How we wrongfully classify them and fail to teach many to read. In *Early reading difficulties: Their misclassification and treatment as learning disabilities* (ERS Research Digest, pp. 4–10). Arlington, VA: Educational Research Service.

Applebee, Arthur, & Langer, Judith A. (1987). *How writing shapes thinking: A study of teaching and learning.* Urbana, IL: National Council of Teachers of English.

Artiles, Alfredo J., & Ortiz, Alba A. (Eds.). (2002). *English language learners with special education needs: Identification, assessment, and instruction.* Washington, DC: Center for Applied Linguistics.

Atwell, Nancie. (1987). *In the middle: Writing, reading, and learning with adolescents.* Portsmouth, NH: Boynton/Cook.

Atwell, Nancie. (1997). *In the middle: Writing, reading, and learning with adolescents* (2nd ed.). Portsmouth, NH: Boynton/Cook.

Atwell, Nancie. (1998). *In the middle: New understandings about writing, reading, and learning.* Portsmouth, NH: Heinemann-Boynton/Cook.

Avioli, Joan, & Davis, Bonnie M. (1994). *Literature of migration and immigration: An anthology of curriculum guides for novels, short stories, poetry, biography and drama.* St. Louis, MO: International Education Consortium.

Bailey, Becky. (2000). *Conscious discipline: 7 basic skills for brain smart classroom management.* Oviedo, FL: Loving Guidance.

Banks, James. (1994). *Multiethnic education: Theory and practice* (3rd ed.). Needham, MA: Allyn & Bacon.

Barr, Robert, & Parrett, William. (2003). *Saving our students, saving our schools.* Glenview, IL: Pearson Professional Development.

Beers, Kylene. (2003). *When kids can't read: What teachers can do.* Portsmouth, NH: Heinemann.

Bishop, John. (2003). *Goal setting for students.* St. Louis, MO: Accent on Success.

Blankenstein, Alan M. (2004). *Failure is NOT an option: Six principles that guide student achievement in high-performing schools.* Thousand Oaks, CA: Corwin.

Bomer, Randy. (1995). *Time for meaning: Crafting literate lives in middle and high school.* Portsmouth, NH: Heinemann.

Brown, Dave F. (2002). *Becoming a successful urban teacher.* Portsmouth, NH: Heinemann.

Brown v. Board of Education. 347 U.S. 483 (1954) (USSC+).

Burke, Jim. (1999a). *The English teacher's companion: A complete guide to classroom, curriculum, and the profession.* Portsmouth, NH: Boynton/Cook.

Burke, Jim. (1999b). *I hear America reading: Why we read, what we read.* Portsmouth, NH: Heinemann.

Burke, Jim. (2000). *Reading reminders: Tools, tips, and techniques.* Portsmouth, NH: Boynton/Cook.

Burke, Jim. (2001). *Illuminating texts: How to teach students to read the world.* Portsmouth, NH: Heinemann.

Burke, Jim. (2003). *Writing reminders: Tools, tips, and techniques.* Portsmouth, NH: Heinemann.

Caine, Renate Nummela, & Caine, Geoffrey. (1997). *Unleashing the power of perceptual change: The potential of brain-based teaching.* Alexandria, VA: ASCD.

Calkins, Lucy. (1986). *The art of teaching writing.* Portsmouth, NH: Heinemann.

Calkins, Lucy, Montgomery, Kate, & Santman, Donna, with Beverly Falk. (1998). *A teacher's guide to standardized reading tests: Knowledge is power.* Portsmouth, NH: Heinemann.

Cameron, Julia. (1992). *The artist's way: A spiritual path to higher creativity.* New York: Putnam.

Carbo, Marie. (1994). Sharply increasing the reading ability of potential dropouts. In Robert C. Morris (Ed.), *Using what we know about at-risk youth: Lessons from the field* (pp. 129–138). Lancaster, PA: Technomic.

Card, Orson Scott. (1985). *Enders game.* New York: Tom Doherty.

Carlson, G. Robert, & Sherrill, Anne. (1988). *Voices of readers: How we come to love books.* Urbana, IL: National Council of Teachers of English.

Carlson, Lori. (Ed.). (1994). *Cool salsa: Bilingual poems on growing up Latino in the United States.* New York: Henry Holt.

Chall, Jeanne S., & Curtis, Mary E. (1992). Teaching the disabled or below-average reader. In S. Jay Samuels & Alan E. Farstrup (Eds.), *What research has to say about reading instruction* (2nd ed., pp. 253–276). Newark, DE: International Reading Association.

Chambers, Aiden. (1985). *Booktalk.* London: Bodley Head.

Christenbury, Leila. (1994). *Making the journey: Being and becoming a teacher of English language arts.* Portsmouth, NH: Boynton/Cook.

Cisneros, Sandra. (1989). *The House on Mango Street.* New York: Random House.

Cisneros, Sandra. (1991). *Woman Hollering Creek and other stories.* New York: Random House.

Cofer, Judith Ortiz. (1995). *An island like you.* New York: Penguin.

Cole, Robert. (Ed.). (1995). *Educating everybody's children: Diverse teaching strategies for diverse learners.* Alexandria, VA: ASCD.

Cole, Robert. (2001). *More strategies for educating everybody's children.* Alexandria, VA: ASCD.

College Board's National Task Force on Minority Achievement. (1999). *Reaching the top: A report of the National Task Force on Minority High Achievement.* New York: Author.

Collins, Kathy. (2004). *Growing readers: Units of study in the primary classroom.* Portland, ME: Stenhouse.

Compton-Lilly, Catherine. (2004). *Confronting racism, poverty, and power: Classroom Strategies to Change the World.* Portsmouth, NH: Heinemann.

Covey, Stephen R. (1989). *The seven habits of highly effective people.* New York: Simon & Schuster.

Csikszentmihalyi, Mihaly. (1991). *Flow: The psychology of optimal experience.* New York: HarperPerennial.

Culham, Ruth. (2003). *6+1 traits of writing.* Portland, OR: Northwest Regional Educational Laboratory.

Cunningham, Patricia M. (2000). *Phonics they use: Words for reading and writing.* New York: Longman.

Cunningham, Patricia, & Allington, Richard. (1999). *Classrooms that work: They can all read and write.* New York: Longman.

Daniels, Harvey, & Bizar, Marilyn. (2005). *Teaching the best practices way: Methods that matter, K–12.* Portland, ME: Stenhouse.

Darling-Hammond, Linda. (1997). *The right to learn: A blueprint for creating schools that work.* San Francisco: Jossey-Bass.

Davidson, Judith, & Koppenhaver, David. (1993). *Adolescent literacy: What works and why.* New York: Garland.

Davis, Bonnie M. (1988). *A rationale for the reconstruction of the American literary canon.* Unpublished dissertation, St. Louis University, St. Louis, MO.

Davis, Bonnie M. (1989). Feminizing the English curriculum: An international perspective. *English Journal, 78*(6).

Davis, Bonnie M. (Ed.). (1990). *Freedom rising: Viewer guide to video production.* St. Louis, MO: Voluntary Interdistrict Council.

Davis, Bonnie M. (1994). A cultural safari: Dispelling myths and creating connections through multicultural and international education. *English Journal, 83*(2).

Davis, Bonnie M. (1996). Writing across the ages: A working writer's workshop. *English Journal, 85*(1).

Davis, Bonnie M. (1997). Radio raincoat man: A state hospital mental patient. *100 Words, 4*(5).

Davis, Bonnie M. (1999). Women in Faulkner's novels. In Robert W. Hamblin & Charles A. Peek (Eds.), *A William Faulkner encyclopedia.* Westport, CT: Greenwood Press.

Delgado, Richard, & Stefancic, Jean. (Eds.). (1997). *Critical White studies: Looking behind the mirror.* Philadelphia: Temple University Press.

Delpit, Lisa. (1995). *Other people's children: Cultural conflict in the classroom.* New York: New Press.

Delpit, Lisa. (1997). Ebonics and cultural responsive instruction. *Rethinking Schools: An Urban Educational Journal, 12*(1).

Dodge, Liz, & Whaley, Liz. (1993). *Weaving in the women: Transforming the high school English curriculum.* Portsmouth, NH: Boynton/Cook.

Dornan, Reade, Rosen, Lois Matz, & Wilson, Marilyn. (1997). *Multiple voices, multiple texts: Reading in the secondary content areas.* Portsmouth, NH: Boynton/Cook.

Draper, Sharon. (1994). *Tears of a tiger.* New York: Simon & Schuster.

Draper, Sharon. (1997). *Forged by fire.* New York: Simon & Schuster.

Ecroyd, Catherine Ann. (1991). Motivating students through reading aloud. *English Journal, 80*(6), 76–78.

Educational Research Service. (1999). *Reading at the middle and high school levels: Building active readers across the curriculum.* Arlington, VA: Author.

Ehrenreich, Barbara. (2001). *Nickel and dimed: On (not) getting by in America.* New York: Henry Holt.

Ellison, Ralph. (1952). *Invisible man.* New York: Random House.

Fielding, Linda C., & Pearson, P. David. (1994, February). Reading comprehension: What works. *Educational Leadership, 52,* 62–68.

Fleischman, Paul. (1997). *Seedfolks.* New York: HarperTrophy.

Fleischman, Paul. (1998). *Whirligig.* New York: Henry Holt.

Fletcher, Ralph. (1996). *Breathing in, breathing out: Keeping a writer's notebook.* Portsmouth, NH: Heinemann.

Fletcher, Ralph, & Portalupi, JoAnn. (1998). *Craft lessons: Teaching writing K–8.* York, ME: Stenhouse.

Fountas, Irene C., & Pinnell, Gay Su. (2001). *Guiding readers and writers, grades 3–6: Teaching comprehension, genre, and content literacy.* Portsmouth, NH: Heinemann.

Fox, Mem. (2001). *Reading magic: Why reading aloud to our children will change their lives forever.* New York: Harcourt.

Freedman, Sarah W., Simons, Elizabeth R., Kalnin, Julie S., Casareno, Alex, & M-Class Teams. (1999). *Inside city schools: Investigating literacy in multicultural classrooms.* Urbana, IL: NCTE.

Freire, Paulo. (2000). *Pedagogy of the oppressed* (30th anniv. ed.). New York: Continuum International.

Freire, Paulo. (2003). *From risk to opportunity: Fulfilling the educational needs of Hispanic Americans in the 21st century* (Final report of the president's advisory commission on educational excellence for Hispanic Americans). Retrieved from http://www.YesICan.gov/paceea/finalreport.pdf

Gallagher, Kelly. (2004). *Deeper reading: Comprehending challenging texts, 4–12.* Portland, ME: Stenhouse.

Gardner, Howard. (1983). *Frames of mind. The theory of multiple intelligences.* New York: Basic.

Gates, Henry Louis, Jr. (1992). *Loose canons: Notes on the culture wars.* New York: Oxford University Press.

Gilligan, Carol. (1982). *In a different voice: Psychological theory and women's development.* Cambridge, MA: Harvard University Press.

Giroux, H. A. (1997). *Pedagogy and the politics of hope: Theory, culture, and schooling.* Boulder, CO: Westview.

Glasser, William A. (1990). *Quality school: Managing students without coercion.* New York: HarperCollins.

Goleman, Daniel. (1995). *Emotional intelligence.* New York: Bantam.

Gonzalez, Maria Luisa, Huerta-Macias, Ana, & Tinajero, Josefina Villamil. (1998). *Educating Latino students: A guide to successful practice.* Lancaster, PA: Technomic.

Graves, Donald H. (1989). *Experiment with fiction.* Portsmouth, NH: Heinemann.

Graves, Donald H. (2002). *Testing is not teaching: What should count in education.* Portsmouth, NH: Heinemann.

Gregory, Gayle, & Chapman, Carolyn. (2002). *Differentiated instructional strategies: One size doesn't fit all.* Thousand Oaks, CA: Corwin.

Gruwell, Erin. (1999). *The freedom writers diary: How a teacher and 150 teens used writing to change themselves and the world around them.* New York: Doubleday.

Haberman, Martin. (1995). *STAR teachers of children in poverty.* West Lafayette, IN: Kappa Delta Pi Biennial.

Haddix, Margaret Peterson. (1998). *Among the hidden.* New York: Simon & Schuster.

Hale, Janice. (2001). *Learning while Black: Creating educational excellence for African-American children.* Baltimore: Johns Hopkins University Press.

Hale-Benson, Janice E. (1986). *Black children: Their roots, culture, and learning styles* (Rev. ed.). Baltimore: Johns Hopkins University Press.

Harvey, Stephanie. (1998). *Nonfiction matters: Reading, writing, and research in grades 3–8.* Portland, ME: Stenhouse.

Haycock, Kati. (2001). Closing the achievement gap. *Educational Leadership, 58*(6).

Henze, Rosemary, Katz, Anne, Norte, Edmundo, Sather, Susan, & Walker, Ernest. (2002). *Leading for diversity: How school leaders promote positive interethnic relations.* Thousand Oaks, CA: Corwin.

Hiller, A. (Director). (1984). *Teachers* [Motion picture]. United States: MGM/United Artists.

Hinojosa, Rolando. (1987). *This migrant earth.* Houston, TX: Arte Publico Press.

Holly, Mary Louise. (1989). *Writing to grow: Keeping a personal-professional journal.* Portsmouth, NH: Heinemann.

Howard, Gary R. (1999). *We can't teach what we don't know: White teachers, multiracial schools.* New York: Teachers College Press.

Hoyt, Linda. (1999). *Revisit, reflect, retell: Strategies for improving reading comprehension.* Portsmouth, NH: Heinemann.

Hoyt, Linda. (2000). *Snapshots: Literacy minilessons up close.* Portsmouth, NH: Heinemann.

Jago, Carol. (2002). *Cohesive writing: Why concept is not enough.* Portsmouth, NH: Heinemann.

Jensen, Eric. (1998). *Teaching with the brain in mind.* Alexandria, VA: ASCD.

Jimenez, Francisco. (1998). *The circuit.* Albuquerque: University of New Mexico Press.

Johnson, Ruth S. (2002). *Using data to close the achievement gap: How to measure equity in our schools.* Thousand Oaks, CA: Corwin.

Keene, Ellin Oliver, & Zimmermann, Susan. (1997). *Mosaic of thought: Teaching comprehension in a reader's workshop.* Portsmouth, NH: Heinemann.

Killens, John Oliver, & Ward, Jerry W., Jr. (Eds.). (1992). *Black southern voices: An anthology of fiction, poetry, drama, nonfiction, and critical essays.* New York: Penguin.

Koppelman, Susan. (1996). *Women in the trees: U.S. women's short stories about battering & resistance, 1839–1994.* Boston: Beacon Press.

Kozol, Jonathon. (1991). *Savage inequalities.* New York: Crown.

Krogness, Mary Mercer. (1995). *Just teach me, Mrs. K: Talking, reading, and writing with resistant adolescent learners.* Portsmouth, NH: Heinemann.

Kunjufu, Jawaanza. (1988). *To be popular or smart: The Black peer group.* Chicago: African-American Images.

Ladson-Billings, Gloria. (1994). *The dreamkeepers: Successful teachers of African American children.* San Francisco: Jossey-Bass.

Landsman, Julie. (2001). *A White teacher talks about race.* Lanham, MD: Scarecrow Press.

Lane, Barry. (1993). *After the end: Teaching and learning creative revision.* Portsmouth, NH: Heinemann.

Langer, Judith. (1995). *Envisioning literature: Literary understanding and literature instruction.* New York: Teachers College Press.

Lee, Stacey J. (1996). *Unraveling the "model minority" stereotype: Listening to Asian American youth.* New York: Teachers College Press.

Levine, Mel. (2002). *A mind at a time: America's top learning expert shows how every child can succeed.* New York: Simon & Schuster.

Lindsey, Randall B., Nuri Robins, Kikanza, & Terrell, Raymond D. (2003). *Cultural proficiency: A manual for school leaders.* Thousand Oaks, CA: Corwin.

Lindsey, Randall B., Roberts, Laraine M., & CampbellJones, Franklin. (2005). *The culturally proficient school: An implementation guide for school leaders.* Thousand Oaks, CA: Corwin.

Long, Michael, & Richards, Jack. (Eds.). (1987). *Methodology in TESOL: A book of readings.* Boston: Heinle & Heinle.

Macrorie, Ken. (1984). *Writing to be read.* Upper Montclair, NJ: Boynton/Cook.

Martinez, Victor. (1998). *Parrot in the oven: Mi vida.* New York: HarperTrophy.

Marzano, Robert. (2003). *Classroom management that works.* Alexandria, VA: ASCD.

Marzano, Robert. (2004). *Building background knowledge for academic achievement.* Alexandria, VA: ASCD.

Marzano, Robert, & Kendall, John S. (1997). *Content knowledge: A compendium of standards and benchmarks for K–12 education* (2nd ed.). Alexandria, VA: ASCD.

Marzano, Robert, Pickering, Debra J., & Pollock, Jane E. (2001). *Classroom instruction that works: Research-based strategies for increasing student achievement.* Alexandria, VA: ASCD.

Mathis, Sharon Bell. (1986). *The hundred penny box.* New York: Viking.

McEwan, Elaine K. (2002). *Ten traits of highly effective teachers: How to hire, coach, and mentor successful teachers.* Thousand Oaks, CA: Corwin.

McIntosh, Peggy. (1998). White privilege and male privilege: A personal account of coming to see correspondences through work in women's studies. In M. L. Andersen & P. Hill-Collins (Eds.), *Race, class, and gender: An anthology* (pp. 70–81). Wellesley, MA: Wellesley College Center for Research for Women.

McIntyre, Alice. (1997). *Making meaning of Whiteness: Exploring racial identity with White teachers.* New York: State University of New York Press.

McKissack, Patricia, & McKissack, Fredrick. (1999). *Black hands, white sails: The story of African-American whalers.* New York: Scholastic.

Medina, Jane. (1999). *My name is Jorge on both sides of the river.* Honesdale, PA: Boyds Mills Press.

Mehrabian, Albert. (1990). *Silent messages: Implicit communication of emotions and attitudes.* New York: Wadsworth.

Morrison, Toni. (1987). *The song of Solomon.* New York: Penguin.

Mowry, J. (1992). *Way past cool.* New York: Farrar, Straus & Giroux.

Murray, Donald. (1985). *A writer teaches writing.* Boston: Houghton Mifflin.

Murray, Donald. (1990). *Shoptalk: Learning to write with writers.* Portsmouth, NH: Boynton/Cook.

Myers, Jim. (2000). *Afraid of the dark: What Whites and Blacks need to know about each other.* Chicago: Lawrence Hill.

Myers, Walter Dean. (1988). *Fast Sam, cool Clyde & stuff.* New York: Viking Press.

Myers, Walter Dean. (1990). *Scorpions.* New York: HarperTrophy.

Myers, Walter Dean. (1991). *Fallen angels.* New York: Scholastic.

Myers, Walter Dean. (1996). *The glory field.* New York: Scholastic.

Myers, Walter Dean. (1998). *Slam.* New York: Scholastic.

Myers, Walter Dean. (1999). *Monster.* New York: HarperCollins.

National Center for Education Statistics. (2000). *NAEP trends in academic achievement.* Washington, DC: U.S. Department of Education.

National Council of Teachers of English/International Reading Association. (1994). *Standards for the assessment of reading and writing.* Urbana, IL: Author.

Nieto, Sonia. (2000). *Affirming diversity: The sociopolitical context of multicultural education* (3rd ed.). Reading, MA: Addison Wesley.

Noguera, Pedro A., & Akom, Antwi. (2000, Summer). The opportunity gap. *The Wilson Quarterly, 24,* 86–87.

Nuri Robins, Kikanza, Lindsey, Randall B., Lindsey, Delores B., & Terrell, Raymond D. (2002). *Culturally proficient instruction: A guide for people who teach.* Thousand Oaks, CA: Corwin.

O'Brien, Tim. (1990). *The things they carried.* Boston: Houghton Mifflin.

Obgu, John. (1991). Immigrant and involuntary minorities in comparative perspective. In John Ogbu & Margaret Gibson (Eds.), *Minority status and schooling.* New York: Garland.

Ogle, Donna. (1986). K-W-L: A teaching model that develops active reading of expository text. *Reading Teacher, 39,* 564–570.

Paley, Grace. (1979). *White teacher.* Cambridge, MA: Harvard University Press.

Palmer, Parker J. (1998). *The courage to teach: Exploring the inner landscape of a teacher's life.* San Francisco: Jossey-Bass.

Papalewis, Rosemary, & Fortune, Rex. (2002). *Leadership on purpose: Promising practices for African American and Hispanic students.* Thousand Oaks, CA: Corwin.

Paulsen, Gary. (1995). *Nightjohn.* New York: Laurel Leaf.

Paulsen, Gary. (1999). *Sarny.* New York: Laurel Leaf.

Pearson, D. P., Rohler, L. R., Dole, J. S., & Duffy, G. G. (1992). Developing expertise in reading comprehension. In S. Jay Samuels & Alan E. Farstrup (Eds.), *What research has to say about reading instruction* (2nd ed.). Newark, DE: International Reading Association.

Peters, Stephen. (2001). *Inspired to learn: Why we must give children hope.* Marietta, GA: Rising Sun.

Portalupi, JoAnn, & Fletcher, Ralph. (2001). *Nonfiction craft lessons: Teaching information writing K–8.* Portland, ME: Stenhouse.

Ratekin, Ned, Simpson, Michele, Alvermann, Donna E., & Dishner, Ernest K. (1985). Why teachers resist content reading instruction. *Journal of Reading, 28*(5), 432–437.

Reglin, Gary. (1995). *Achievement for African-American students: Strategies for the diverse classroom.* Bloomington, IN: National Education Service.

Rico, Gabriele Lusser. (1983). *Writing the natural way: Using right-brain techniques to release your expressive powers.* Los Angeles: J. P. Tarcher.

Rief, Linda. (1992). *Seeking diversity: Language arts with adolescents.* Portsmouth, NH: Heinemann.

Rief, Linda. (1998). *Vision and voice: Extending the literacy spectrum.* Portsmouth, NH: Heinemann.

Robb, Laura, Nauman, April, & Ogle, Donna. (2002). *Reader's handbook: A student guide for reading and learning.* Wilmington, MA: Great Source.

Rodriguez, L. (1993). *Always running.* Willimantic, CT: Curbstone Press.

Romano, Tom. (1987). *Clearing the way: Working with teenage writers.* Portsmouth, NH: Heinemann.

Rosenblatt, Louise. (1995). *Literature as exploration* (5th ed.). New York: Modern Language Association of America.

Routman, Regie. (2000). *Conversation: Strategies for teaching, learning, and evaluating.* Portsmouth, NH: Heinemann.

Sachar, Louis. (1998). *Holes.* New York: Farrar, Straus & Giroux.

Santa, Carol M. (1988). Changing teacher behavior in content reading through collaborative research. In S. Jay Samuels & P. David Pearson (Eds.), *Changing school reading programs: Principles and case studies* (pp. 185–206). Newark, DE: International Reading Association.

Senge, Peter. (2000). *Schools that learn: A fifth discipline fieldbook for educators, parents, and everyone who cares about education.* New York: Doubleday-Currency.

Shange, Ntozake. (1985). *Betsey Brown.* New York: Picador.

Sherman, Charlotte Watson. (1994). *Sisterfire: Black womanist fiction and poetry.* New York: HarperPerennial.

Silven, M., &. Vauras, M. (1992). Improving reading through thinking aloud. *Learning and Instruction, 2*(2), 69–88.

Silver, H. F., Strong, R. W., & Perini, M. J. (2000). *So each may learn: Integrating learning styles and multiple intelligences.* Alexandria, VA: ASCD.

Singham, Mano. (1998). The canary in the mine: The achievement gap between Black and White students. *Kappan, 80*(1), 9–15.

Singleton, Glen. (2003, August 12–13). *De-institutionalizing racism.* Workshop. Cooperating School Districts, University of Missouri, St. Louis, MO.

Singleton, Glenn E., & Linton, Curtis. (2006). *Courageous conversations about race: A field guide for creating equity in schools.* Thousand Oaks, CA: Corwin.

Sleeter, Christine. (1996). *Multicultural education as social activism.* Albany: State University of New York Press.

Soto, Gary. (1991). *A summer life.* New York: Laurel Leaf.

Soto, Gary. (1992). *Living up the street.* New York: Laurel Leaf.

Soto, Gary. (1992). *Taking sides.* New York: Harcourt.

Soto, Gary. (1993. *Pieces of the heart: New Chicano fiction.* New York: Chronicle.

Soto, Gary. (1995). *New and selected poems.* New York: Chronicle.

Soto, Gary. (1997). *Junior college.* New York: Chronicle.

Soto, Gary. (1999). *Buried onions.* New York: HarperTrophy.

Sousa, David. (2001). *How the brain learns.* Thousand Oaks, CA: Corwin.

Spinelli, Jerry. (2000). *Stargirl.* New York: Random House.

Steele, Claude. (1999). Thin ice: "Stereotype threat" and Black college students. *Atlantic Monthly, 284*(2).

Stone, Randi. (2002). *Best practices for high school classrooms: What award-winning secondary teachers do.* Thousand Oaks, CA: Corwin.

Sylwester, Robert. (2000). *A biological brain in a cultural classroom: Applying biological research to classroom management.* Thousand Oaks, CA: Corwin.

Tannen, Deborah. (1990). *You just don't understand: Men and women in conversation.* New York: Ballantine.

Tate, Marcia L. (2003). *Worksheets don't grow dendrites: Instructional strategies that engage the brain.* Thousand Oaks, CA: Corwin.

Tate, Marcia L. (2004). *"Sit and get" won't grow dendrites: 20 professional learning strategies that engage the adult brain.* Thousand Oaks, CA: Corwin.

Tatum, Beverly Daniel. (1997). *Why are all the Black kids sitting together in the cafeteria?* New York: Basic Books.

Taylor, Kathe, & Walton, Sherry. (1998). *Children at the center: A workshop approach to standardized test preparation, K–8.* Portsmouth, NH: Heinemann.

Thornton, Yvonne S. (1995). *The ditchdigger's daughters: A Black family's astonishing success story.* New York: Penguin.

Tileston, Donna Walker. (2004). *What every teacher should know about diverse learners.* Thousand Oaks, CA: Corwin.

Tomlinson, Carol Ann. (1999). *The differentiated classroom: Responding to the needs of all learners.* Alexandria, VA: ASCD.

Tomlinson, Carol Ann. (2003). *Fulfilling the promise of the differentiated classroom: Strategies and tools for responsive teaching.* Alexandria, VA: ASCD.

Tovani, Cris. (2000). *I read it, but I don't get it: Comprehension strategies for adolescent readers.* Portland, ME: Stenhouse.

Tovani, Cris. (2004). *Do I really have to teach reading?: Content comprehension, grades 6–12.* Portland, ME: Stenhouse.

Trueman, Terry. (2000). *Stuck in neutral.* New York: HarperCollins.

Tsujimoto, Joseph. (2001). *Lighting fires: How the passionate teacher engages adolescent writers.* Portsmouth, NH: Heinemann.

Veljkovic, Peggy, & Schwartz, Arthur J. (Eds.). (2001). *Writing from the heart: Young people share their wisdom.* Philadelphia: Templeton Foundation Press.

Viadero, Debra. (2000). Bridging the gap. *Teacher,* May/June.

Vygotsky, Lev. (1994). *Thought and language* (A. Kosulin, Trans. & Ed.). Cambridge: MIT Press.

Walker, Alice. (1983). *In search of our mother's gardens.* New York: Harcourt Brace Jovanovich.

Ward, Jerry. (Ed.). (1997). *Trouble the water: 250 years of African-American poetry.* New York: Putnam.

Wiggins, Grant, & McTighe, Jay. (1998). *Understanding by design.* Alexandria, VA: ASCD.

Wilhelm, Jeffrey D. (1995). *"You gotta be the book": Teaching engaged and reflective reading with adolescents.* New York: Teachers College Press.

Williams, Belinda. (Ed.). (1996). *Closing the achievement gap: A vision for changing beliefs and practices.* Alexandria, VA: ASCD.

Williams, Lena. (2002). *It's the little things: The everyday interactions that anger, annoy, and divide the races.* New York: Harcourt.

Wong, Harry K., & Wong, Rosemary Tripi. (1998). *The first day of school: How to be an effective teacher* (Rev. ed.). Mountain View, CA: Harry K. Wong.

Woodbury, Jacqueline. (1997). No more rules! Simplify your discipline plan with these five statements. *Learning,* November/December.

Wynn, Mychal. (1992). *Empowering African-American males to succeed: A ten-step approach for parents and teachers.* Marietta, GA: Rising Sun.

Zeni, Jane, Krater, Joan, & Cason, Nancy Devlin. (1994). *Mirror images: Teaching writing in black and white.* Action research from the Webster Groves Writing Project. Portsmouth, NH: Heinemann.

Index

Facilitator's Guide

This is a Facilitator's Guide to Professional Development Activities/Sessions, divided by district educator roles and/or time frames.

Level/Subject: Adult (Cross-curricular)

Standards: National Staff Development Council Standards (NSDC)

Context Standards: Learning communities. Staff development that improves the learning of all students organizes adults into learning communities whose goals are aligned with those of the school and district.

Process Standards: Collaboration. Staff development that improves the learning of all students provides educators with the knowledge and skills to collaborate.

Content Standards: Equity. Staff development that improves the learning of all students prepares educators to understand and appreciate all students, create safe, orderly, and supportive learning environments, and hold high expectations for their academic achievement.

As mentioned in the preface, this book was written to be read and responded to chapter by chapter in a planned sequence that takes the reader through the following stages: first, a general recognition of one's culture and an understanding of the particular needs of and research about diverse learners; second, an exploration of our inner world with an examination of racism and its impact upon our daily lives; third, strategies for establishing a school climate in which to teach diverse learners; fourth, research-based instructional strategies to implement across the disciplines, with a focus on literacy development; and finally, a model for an academic support group for diverse learners and suggestions for professional development.

However, some educators may find chapters and/or sections that meet the immediate needs of staff and may choose to use particular sections in set time frames. This quick guide gives you multiple suggestions for using the book in your district setting.

Note: This book can be used in preservice or graduate classes as part of a unit or course on diverse learners. Currently, it is used at Fontbonne University in St. Louis, Missouri, for a course on diverse learners.

I. Developed for administrators, staff developers, professional development chairs (PDCs), professional learning communities, teacher leaders, and department heads.

    Suggested time frame: One-hour or 90-minute workshop format.

A. Chapter 1: "Our Culture: The Way We View the World." Use in a 60- or 90-minute format with a facilitator to guide participants through the reflections and discussion. The chapter includes several strategies to address cultural proficiency as well as a planning page for actual steps to take to counteract discrimination. Use at the onset of a school year or the beginning of a staff's journey as they investigate cultural proficiency and the diversity of their student body.

B. Part III, Chapters 7, 8, and 9: "Creating a Learning Environment That Supports Diverse Learners." These chapters examine how we work together as a staff or in a classroom as we build a rigorously academic school culture. Assign your staff these chapters and discuss them at a meeting. Use these chapters with a department as they begin their year's work together. For example, at the first English department meeting of the year, have the department members discuss these three chapters as they set norms and expectations for the school and for their interactions with each other. End with a discussion of how staff can welcome students and parents/caregivers, using the suggestions and strategies in Part III that include relationships and school culture.

C. Chapter 10: "Cultivating Relationships With Diverse Learners." Use this chapter to reinforce the research that stresses the need for a relationship between the diverse learner and the teacher and the necessity for building a community in which the diverse learner can thrive. This chapter is full of strategies to build relationships and create community. Have staff discuss these strategies as well as additional successful strategies they currently use.

II. Developed for administrators, staff developers.

    Suggested time frame: Two-hour-plus sessions.

A. Chapter 9: "Using Books to Support School and Community Partnerships." Team-building activity (approximately two hours or more). This chapter is designed to be used as a staff development activity, community book experience, or a classroom lesson. If used with a staff, you can complete this chapter in three hours. With your community group, you may use this in an evening session. With students, you would use this chapter with your study of the novel; the time you spend will vary depending upon your instructional design.

B. Chapter 3: "What We Know About the Achievement Gap." This chapter takes two hours or more to present thoroughly and discuss. You may want to divide the achievement gap theories into two groups: those we educators can influence and those mostly out of our control. Also, if possible, use the articles cited in the headings to each gap theory to enrich this information and provide additional information for discussion.

Suggestion: Assign the achievement gap theories to small groups, and have each group investigate a theory and report back at the next staff meeting. Focus on one or two theories per meeting: the root causes, the impact in your school, the research, and successful strategies.

III. Developed for literacy curriculum directors, department heads, literacy teachers, and teachers of English, reading, ELL, and related disciplines (humanities, history courses, etc.).
    Suggested time frame: One hour.

  A. Chapter 14: "Building a Balanced Literacy Classroom: Reading and Writing Workshops." Use this chapter as a model for readers and writers workshops at any level. It illustrates how the principles of powerful reading and writing workshops cross grade levels. Have literacy staff read and then discuss this chapter.

  B. Chapter 15: "Differentiating Instruction." This chapter contains several lesson plan ideas for middle school and high school students. Literacy staff can read and discuss at a department meeting.

IV. Developed for staff study groups, professional learning communities, and individuals.
    Suggested time frame: One hour.

  A. Chapter 16: "Multidisciplinary Experiences." This chapter includes class and schoolwide experiences (cross-curricular) that motivate and include diverse learners into the large school community. Share this at a faculty meeting or in a professional learning community and discuss how staff might implement these suggested academic experiences.

  B. Chapter 11: "Reaching Diverse Learners Through Strategic Instruction." (Cross-curricular.) This chapter explores powerful teaching strategies based on the research of David Sousa, Robert Marzano, Marcia Tate, and others. Use this chapter on a professional development day with a facilitator to acquaint teachers with these strategies, providing time for teacher practice and planning.

V. Developed for intensive self-study or for groups prepared to examine racism.
    Suggested time frame: Two hours each.

  A. Chapter 5: "Exploring our Racial Identity" and Chapter 6: "A Day in the Life . . ." These two chapters examine racism and its impact on our daily lives. Use these two chapters with a trained facilitator or in a book study with participants who have volunteered to examine this issue. Use Chapter 5 for one meeting (approximately two hours, depending on the number of participants). Invite participants to write their racial histories and share in pairs or groups. A facilitator can process the sharing and support participants as they list the commonalities and dissimilarities among group members' racial histories. Draw conclusions and, if possible, reach consensus as to the impact of diverse racial histories upon our work together at a school setting.

B. Use Chapter 6 at a subsequent meeting. Have participants write a similar "day in the life . . ." and share. Discuss and plan how best to accommodate the needs of all members of the school community based on what was learned about the impact of race upon staff members' daily lives.

VI. Developed for self-study or for use by administrators, professional learning communities, department heads, evaluators, and professional development chairs.

Suggested time frame: Varies, depending upon chosen application.

A. Chapter 4: "Reflecting on the Educator Self." This chapter includes a list of questions that invite reflection. Divide the list among participants, having them work in pairs, small groups, or alone. These questions might serve as a guide to use throughout the year (ask staff to answer one or two per month). Use each one separately as a writing prompt to begin staff or department meetings. Staff could keep their reflections in a professional journal or logbook, which could become part of their professional development plan or evaluation.

VII. Developed for administrators, professional development chairs, teacher leaders, learning communities, and staff.

A. Facilitator's Guide

B. Selected Bibliography

BOOK STUDY GROUPS: SUGGESTED BOOKS

Level/Subject: Adult (Cross-curricular)

Standards: National Staff Development Council Standards (NSDC)

Context standards: Learning communities; leadership; resources

Process standards: Data driven; evaluation; research based; design; learning; collaboration

Content: Equity; quality teaching; family involvement

Book study groups are a powerful way for educators to learn together. Staff can choose to meet weekly or monthly in the morning or afternoon. In one elementary school, we met before school once a month. Participants took turns bringing snacks and facilitating the discussion. We all looked forward to the lively discussion and the yummy food. At a middle school, the principal provided coffee, juice, and rolls every other week as we met and discussed classroom management (using Becky Bailey's 2001 book, *Conscious Discipline*). At a high school, we met after school once a month, our tables filled with

FACILITATOR'S GUIDE

chocolate and other goodies. When using this book, we usually assign a chapter or two each time and discuss it informally in sessions. For more challenging books focusing on race, you may want to use an outside facilitator for your group. Set group guidelines for your discussions and pay close attention to those focusing on "airtime" and use of language.

These are suggested books to use in book study groups with educators to heighten their awareness of the needs and potentials of diverse learners (see full citations in the Selected Bibliography).

Artiles, Alfredo J., and Alba A. Ortiz, eds. 2002. *English Language Learners With Special Education Needs.*

Bailey, Becky. 2001. *Conscious Discipline: 7 Basic Skills for Brain Smart Classroom Management.*

Delpit, Lisa. 1995. *Other People's Children: Cultural Conflict in the Classroom.*

Gonzalez, Maria Luisa, et al. 1998. *Educating Latino Students: A Guide to Successful Practice.*

Henze, Rosemary, et al. 2002. *Leading for Diversity: How School Leaders Promote Positive Interethnic Relations.*

Howard, Gary R. 1999. *We Can't Teach What We Don't Know: White Teachers, Multiracial Schools.*

Johnson, Ruth S. 2002. *Using Data to Close the Achievement Gap: How to Measure Equity in Our Schools.*

Kunjufu, Jawaanza. 1988. *To Be Popular or Smart: The Black Peer Group.*

Ladson-Billings, Gloria. 1994. *The Dreamkeepers: Successful Teachers of African American Children.*

Landsman, Julie. 2001. *A White Teacher Talks About Race.*

Lee, Stacey J. 1996. *Unraveling the "Model Minority" Stereotype: Listening to Asian American Youth.*

Levine, Mel. 2002. *A Mind at a Time: America's Top Learning Expert Shows How Every Child Can Succeed.*

Lindsey, Randall, et al. 2003. *Cultural Proficiency: A Manual for School Leaders.*

Lindsey, Randall, et al. 2005. *The Culturally Proficient School: An Implementation Guide for School Leaders.*

Long, Michael, and Jack Richards, eds. 1987. *Methodology in TESOL: A Book of Readings.*

McIntyre, Alice. 1997. *Making Meaning of Whiteness: Exploring Racial Identity With White Teachers.*

Nuri Robins, Kikanza, et al. 2002. *Culturally Proficient Instruction: A Guide for People Who Teach.*

Singleton, Glenn, and Curtis Linton. 2006. *Courageous Conversations About Race.*

Tatum, Beverly Daniel. 1997. *Why Are All the Black Kids Sitting Together in the Cafeteria?*

Tileston, Donna Walker. 2004. *What Every Teacher Should Know About Diverse Learners.*

Williams, Belinda, ed. 1996. *Closing the Achievement Gap: A Vision for Changing Beliefs and Practices.*

❖   ❖   ❖

We read in order to gain new information and insight. With this new information and insight, we can examine our instructional practices and our perceptions of reality. What books have caused you to rethink your instructional practices? In what ways did you change your classroom instruction? What books caused you to question your reality? In what ways did you change your perceptions of reality?

_____

_____

_____

_____

Suggest books for your colleagues.

_____

_____

_____

_____

_____

_____

_____

**CORWIN
PRESS**

The Corwin Press logo—a raven striding across an open book—represents the union of courage and learning. Corwin Press is committed to improving education for all learners by publishing books and other professional development resources for those serving the field of PreK–12 education. By providing practical, hands-on materials, Corwin Press continues to carry out the promise of its motto: **"Helping Educators Do Their Work Better."**